KARL MARX
The Roots of His Thought

JOHAN VAN DER HOEVEN
Free University/Amsterdam

KARL MARX
The Roots of His Thought

WEDGE PUBLISHING FOUNDATION/TORONTO 1976

Wedge Publishing Foundation, 229 College Street, Toronto, Canada M5T 1R4

ISBN 0-88906-001-0

Printed in The Netherlands by Van Gorcum, Assen.

To my wife Joke and our boys

SUMMARY OF CONTENTS

CHAPTER IV   MARX'S „CONTRIBUTION TO THE CRITIQUE OF HEGEL'S PHILOSOPHY OF RIGHT"

CHAPTER V   MARX'S ECONOMIC & PHILOSOPHIC MANUSCRIPTS

CHAPTER VI   SOME KEY NOTIONS OF MARX

EPILOGUE

FOREWORD

The content of this book is the subject matter of a course of lectures I gave in 1971 as guest lecturer at Calvin College, Grand Rapids, Michigan. Apart from a number of absolutely necessary corrections, the lectures are here published as they were originally given. Publishing a book in this lecture form brings with it, however, several evident drawbacks.

First of all there are the inevitable repetitions. Next, the emphasis of exercising and schooling students in the Marxian dialectical thought and its background must override that of strict, systematic-analytical exposition. Perhaps there are readers, however, who see in this special advantages of its own.

Furthermore, after the introductory part, the discussion of Marx follows, for the greater part, a textual-analytical method. I am persuaded, for more than one reason, of the value of such a procedure before a student audience, especially when treating the classic texts of great philosophers. But whether this procedure is appropriate in book form, when reaching a broader circle of readers, I dare not say.

In any case, this publication has no pretensions of being a "study" of Marx in the sense professional philosophers attach to that word.

I can only hope that the book, despite the above-mentioned and other shortcomings, may contribute to a better understanding of and an appropriate confrontation with this great Western "testator".

Finally, I should like to express my thanks to all those who have taken the special trouble of typing out these lectures from taped recordings and giving them a first provisional form; the latter included, not in the last place, correcting my spoken English. I want to mention especially H. der Nederlanden, J.H. Heida, P.B. Hubers, R. Reitsma and J.P. Roberts. I am also indebted to my assistants at the Free University, Drs. John Kraay and Drs. Anthony Tol, who together translated the Epilogue and made many valuable suggestions as well as corrections in the manuscript.

Free University   J. van der Hoeven
Amsterdam

CHAPTER I

The Rise of German Idealism

1. *Kant's Dualistic Critique*

German Idealism was born through critique, through critical enterprise
– one need only think of the titles of the major works of Kant: *The
Critique of Pure Reason, The Critique of Practical Reason* and *The
Critique of Judgement.* In this critical enterprise Kant assimilated two
other critiques and transformed them into critical reflections upon the
very foundations of modern thought. These two other critiques were,
first, the skeptical, psychologically oriented, epistemological critique
of Hume, and secondly, the protest critique of Rousseau, who may be
called the first provo[1] of Western Civilization and of Western philosophy. For Kant this critical enterprise meant that reason examine itself
as to its limits, its tenability and its meaning in order to pass beyond
dogmatic and skeptical thought.

There are two basic questions which Kant asks: the first being, "What
can I know?" and the second, "What ought I to do?" These two basic
questions indicate the double background of Kant's enterprise[2].

1.1.   As to the first question – "What can I know?" – Kant was
deeply impressed by the possibilities and achievements of modern
scientific knowledge, especially by the achievements of Newton in the
natural sciences. But although Newton's results seemed comprehensive
and exact, Kant also had to face Hume's skepticistic critique of the
epistemological foundations of knowledge. The latter, if valid, was
bound to bring into question the reliability of the natural sciences.

---

[1] The provo movement was a valiant youth movement in the Netherlands which
today has merged with various other movements.
[2] There is also a third basic question, and even a fourth one, namely (3) "What may
I hope for?" ("Was darf ich hoffen?") and (4) "What is man?". As to to the third
one, this question is dealt with by Kant in close connection with the second one; we
shall not discuss it in this book. Still, it remains important to mention it as a basic
question, especially in view of the "eschatological" aspects of Marxism and of the
general concern in contemporary thinking for "hope" and "survival". As to the
fourth question, we may consider it to be the ultimate one, into which the other
three converge. This means that Kant wants to be understood as a philosopher who
is concerned with the *human* character of "science" (first question) and of "morality"
(second question).

Hume observed that we believe bread to be nourishing. Why? Because man comes to believe this by *habit* after experiencing repeatedly that bread is nourishing. Although our belief that bread is nourishing is relatively certain, it is not absolutely certain; at best, such a statement remains hypothetical. In fact, matters become even more problematic in that in such a belief as that bread is nourishing we cannot do without memory. But why should memory be reliable as a guide? It obviously fails sometimes or deceives us. It is easy to apply this argument in the field of the natural sciences with destructive consequences for the reliability of the alleged knowledge of the natural sciences. Hume himself did not go that far. He introduced the Laws of Association which guarantee constant relationships in the occurrence of ideas. Nevertheless, the situation remained delicate since these Laws could only be secondary mechanisms: at best able to bring order into the original flux of the many, passing impressions, but unable to cancel them and to guarantee "objective" knowledge.

Thus, Kant was impressed not only by Newton's work but also by the skeptical critique of Hume. Against this general background a basic question arises: How can the foundations of science, especially the natural sciences, be established definitely and with universal validity? At the same time, Kant firmly believed in human freedom and in man's responsibility for his actions, partly as a consequence of his pietistic upbringing and partly from the influence of Rousseau's critique of the intellectualistic, rationalistic culture of the Enlightenment. The protest critique of Rousseau, which deeply impressed Kant, was intended as a rehabilitation of man, especially, of his inborn, ineradicable sense or feeling of freedom, as contrasted with the deterministic, even materialistic tendencies of the Enlightenment culture.

1.2. In an often quoted statement, Kant expresses his debt to Rousseau: "I am a born scholar, but in a way I was converted by Rousseau, otherwise I would sit in my study and study all the time; but when I read Rousseau, I discovered man and I learned to honor man." In the light of this explanation, there arises a second question: How can a well-founded and apparently "closed" science, like Newton's natural science, be connected with and reconciled to a world and life view which demands that a just place be accorded to the freedom of man? With the phrase, "the freedom of man", Kant meant that man is a moral and responsible being. For the sake of brevity, we could label this dual background with the terms "science ideal" and "personality ideal".[3] In doing this, however, we must notice two things.

---

[3] These are terms introduced by H. Dooyeweerd of the Free University of Amsterdam; cf. his *A New Critique of Theoretical Thought*, vol. I, Part II (Philadelphia: Presbyterian and Reformed Publ. Co., 1953), pp. 169-495.

First, the science ideal, prevalent in modern Western philosophy since Galileo, Hobbes and Descartes up to Kant, although present in many interesting variations, had become less self-evident than it had been before Kant. This was so because, as a result of the critiques of Hume and Rousseau, the certainty as well as the range or the extent of this science ideal had become questionable.

1.3. Secondly, in his adoption of the personality ideal, Kant broke with the conceptions of Hume and Rousseau. In their conceptions personality was placed in the sphere of human feeling. This basically psychologistic interpretation Kant rejected, observing that thereby the human personality is treated in a naturalistic manner; in fact, it dissolved it into a complex of habits and customs. Kant saw that this psychologism treated man's "autonomy" either in a naturalistic sense or played it off against reason. The latter possibility is especially evident in Rousseau's sentimentalism. Sentiment is played off against reason, i.e. against the critical testing by reason, which is an universally valid function. Kant was aware of this in Rousseau; for although he was influenced by Rousseau, he was not uncritical toward him. Kant was never to give up this assessment of reason as a critical and universally valid function. Because the execution of the function of reason stands under the direction of the personality and the latter is not psychological, therefore he tried to find a more appropriate place for pure human personality. He thought this place to be in the ethical or moral aspect of human existence and experience.

In this moral sphere certain norms and obligations appeal to man, directly and urgently. These norms cannot be dissolved in a naturalistic manner as in Hume's "moral sense", "feeling of sympathy" and the like. Neither can they be surrendered to an unpredictable flow of sentiment and emotions; for they concern man's most authentic and proper being, confronting him there with universally valid obligations. Human dignity lies precisely in this openness to moral obligation; for it summons man out of his inner being to treat humanity both in himself and others as an *end in itself*, instead of as a means.

1.4. A critical philosophy according to Kant is, first, a philosophy that is not dogmatic. That is, it does not start from self-evident, or would-be self-evident beliefs, statements or presuppositions, but tests and accounts for them, by fixing or stipulating the limits within which certain notions, concepts, statements or beliefs are valid. This is the assignment of a critical philosophy and the first part of the meaning of the word "critical" in Kant's sense. The second part of this meaning is that a critical philosophy is one which surmounts skepticism; for a positive fixing of the limits of reason's validity constitutes a foundation unassailable to skepticistic destruction. Indeed, Kant thought that a destruction, such as Hume's psychological critique, presupposed this same foundation; thus, it is really self-defeating.

1.5. Closely connected with the forementioned term is another which is important in understanding not only Kant but also the true meaning of German Idealism, namely, the term "transcendental". Philosophy for Kant was transcendental in the sense that it should be an investigation into the *a-priori* elements, in human knowledge and experience in general, that underlie all empirical research with its varying and always unfinished gathering of information.

1.6. Here again we must look at the two basic questions. The answer to the first basic question – "What can I know?" – constitutes the so-called Copernican Revolution in epistemology: our ideas and ideals of the certainty and validity of our knowledge no longer have to be tuned to the object of knowledge, but vice versa. The object of our knowledge is dependent on the organization and the structure of our subjective understanding. Nature (reality) only answers the questions we put to it, and we pose these questions as judges, not as pupils. An organization of knowledge exists which is at the same time universally valid[4] and subjective, a knowledge which is knowledge in general. This knowledge basically consists of *a-priori* forms of sense perception and of understanding (intellectual thought).

Kant thought that he had in this way overcome two things: objectivist metaphysics and objectivist epistemology. The general orientation of knowledge had been to "things-in-themselves" (*Ding-an-sich*); there was even a great deal of speculation as to the *properties* of these. Kant thought that he had overcome both this objectivist metaphysics and its negative counterpart, namely, skepticism, which denied that one could know anything whatsoever about things-as-they-are-in-themselves. Kant's conception, however, implied that our truly universally valid knowledge remains limited to the field of possible phenomena, things as they appear to our consicousness. They appear to our consciousness by means of a special organization in the forms of sense perception and forms of understanding. By postulating that our universally valid knowledge is a knowledge which remains limited to the field of phenomena, Kant is no longer compelled to draw skepticistic consequences because he has founded knowledge in subjective organization.

---

[4] By universally valid Kant means holding for all men; subjective thought-organization is common to all men. Kant identifies the structure of the subjective act of knowing with the rules or laws of knowledge which hold for the acquiring of knowledge. It is not only *descriptive* but is also *prescriptive*. That is really what the word autonomy means: I myself am the law. This humanistic view of man's place in reality lies behind Kant's Copernican Revolution. In Kant it is only partially expressed, for although he cannot really sustain it in all respects, it is, nevertheless, his general principle.

Nevertheless, Kant continues to speak about the things-in-themselves, not in order to speculate, but because he too could not dismiss the thing-in-itself, for his thought was still embedded in a form-matter scheme — a tenacious scheme descending from the Greeks. Thus, Kant settled the question of certainty and of universal validity in a new way by pointing to an *a-priori* organization of knowledge in man himself; but this organization consisted of forms of sense perception and forms of understanding.

1.7. This resulted in a further complication also associated with this form-matter scheme. Kant stressed the importance of sense perception. The reliability of the sense element in our knowledge rests upon these *a-priori* forms of sense perception. This conflicts with the interpretation of sense perception in terms of separate and passing sense data, for the forms of sense perception are time and space.

Beside these forms of sense perception exist the forms of understanding which actually begin to assume the greater importance in Kant's thought. This is only natural, since to Kant the formative activity of the knowing subject is here much more pronounced and clear: he speaks of concept formation rather than sense formation. Compared with the formative function of intellectual understanding, sensation and sense perception represent the more receptive and passive side of human knowledge; they merely supply the material necessary to serve the intellectual form-ation of concepts.

1.8. Although Kant stresses the *a-priori* forms, he still needs a material complement to these forms of sense perception. Here the thing-in-itself no longer functions as a thing of metaphysical speculation, but as the final source of this sensory material. Without a thing-in-itself, despite the little we know about it, Kant would be unable to explain the origin of the sensory material. This duality and tension persisted in Kantian Idealism and occasioned further developments in German, post-Kantian Idealism.

1.9. Another duality closely connected to Kant's second basic question (i.e., what ought I to do?) also occasioned further developments in post-Kantian philosophy. And it turned out to be an even more unorthodox position. This is the complementary side to Kant's Copernican Revolution in epistemology. Through the latter he could limit our scientific knowledge to phenomena. Kant did not mean this limitation in a negative or a skepticistic sense; but in showing the limits of scientific knowledge, he meant to disclose to us another, a different perspective. Kant has made room in order to enable us to freely acknowledge with a clean rational conscience the true or the ultimate things-in-themselves. Now that scientific knowledge has been established but limited to phenomena, we may acknowledge those things which are truly ultimate: namely, the reality of the soul, i.e., moral being; the reality of the world as a whole, i.e., the society of the souls of moral beings; and, finally, the reality of God. To Kant God is the guarantor of moral order and of rewards in a future life to those who have kept up to the prescriptions of their moral conscience despite the lack of a concomitant experience of happiness proportionate to their moral efforts. These are the three varieties of things-in-themselves for which Kant made room in his limitation of scientific knowledge. And in terms of these he formulates that basic motive of human freedom, which we discussed above, in order to be able, finally, to found free personality in them. Thus, these three ideas are basic to the reality of free and responsible human life. After the foundation and the limits of valid scientific knowledge have been established, there is no longer any reason to deny these realities, or to confuse them by means of the inappropriate would-be scientific approach of traditional metaphysics.

Thus, Kant could acknowledge these ultimate realities of the soul, the world and God, and to a certain extent even dealt with them, rationally, namely, with our so-called practical reason. However, this position still implies a duality; for the field of pure reason, which is responsible for universally valid knowledge, and the field of practical reason, which has to deal with moral matters, remain separate fields. Kant made different attempts to bridge this gulf, but it has been recognized that these attempts were not very successful – they could not be successful. Kant could not rid himself of this bifurcation because he needed it to keep scientific knowledge and its alleged universality clear, while keeping moral freedom and human responsibility pure. Here the nature-freedom polarity, as Kant himself called it, asserts itself.

1.10. Kant's struggle with this problem also carried over into the sphere of moral freedom. There the same form-matter scheme displays a similarly pervasive influence; in fact, it is even more striking there. Moral obligation is the basic characteristic of our deepest self; it expresses itself in what Kant calls the "categorical imperative". The term "categorical", in this connection, is meant to be an unconditioned sign of human dignity in the moral sphere.

Although we should not forget what was said about the *a-priori* forms, in the science of nature, of natural phenomena, events remain dependent on the on-going stream of experience. Thus, in dealing with it, we cannot do without many hypothetical statements, that is, statements with a condition, a proviso; for in our experience of nature we receive matter that is never fully intelligible or intellectually predictable. In contrast, categorical means non-hypothetical, unconditionally valid, transcending the lower sphere of the senses and sensuous inclinations. We are now able to visualize the implications of Kant's entire conception. "Categorical" becomes, at one and the same time, purely formal, empty of all material content, an abstract "ought", and also a sign of human dignity. But the two do not merge into a synthesis. The categorical imperative must prove its worth in confrontation with and continual subjugation of the sensuous inclinations. There is also a more elaborate formulation of the moral imperative, which is: "Act in such a way as if the maxim of your actions could become by your will a general law of nature". This constitutes our moral freedom and therefore our human dignity. We must conclude, however, that this explication of human autonomy also turns out to be a rather formalistic freedom. It also betrays his orientation to the laws of nature which are the domain of science.

2. *The Idealist Attempt at Synthesis after Kant*

The last observation has direct relevance to the chief issues of post-Kantian Idealism, specifically, of Fichte, Schelling and Hegel. In order to demonstrate this relevance, we must first trace our previously identified dual motive which we called the science ideal and the personality ideal through post-Kantian Idealism. Here we encounter a final grand attempt at synthesizing into one all-encompassing system these two motives. In this synthesis, idealists tried to do justice to the free spirit or mind (*Geist*)[5] in the totality of its mobility and many-sidedness: this is the personality ideal. On the other hand, they wanted to conceptualize this free spirit in its mobility and many-sidedness, to grasp it in the manner of conceptual and logical thought; here we again meet with the "science ideal". German idealism tried to achieve this synthesis especially by its interpretation of two key notions: that of history and that of dialectics.

2.1. To the post-Kantian idealists history is, generally speaking, the free spirit or free mind, in other words, the acting ego. Selfhood (or *das Ich*, as Fichte liked to call it) is not given ready-made; it can be itself only by permanently distinguishing itself from itself, that is, by taking distance from itself. Being itself, for this free spirit, means to become itself, to develop, to form, to cultivate itself – thus, a process. One might ask, why not *simply* say, "to be itself is to become itself"? For these Idealists, especially for Hegel, there is more at stake than just a certain possible sense of the word *sein* (to be), namely, *werden* (to become). It also involves more than just a playing off of one aspect of reality over against another: namely, the aspect of *becoming* – change,

---

[5] The German word *Geist*, as it is used by Hegel, has been translated differently, as in the two books of Struik, *The Economic & Philosophic Manuscripts of 1844* and Bottomore, *Karl Marx, Early Writings.* Struik says, "the absolute is MIND," whereas the same passage in Bottomore reads, "the absolute is SPIRIT". The German word *Geist* has these two linguistic usages.

variation and instability – over against the aspect of *being* – constancy, identity and stability.

Hegel really means to say that the being of free spirit is identical with becoming. For the concept of being implies the notion of being-no-more and of being-not-yet. Thus, Hegel concludes that there is an identity of being and non-being, a unity of opposites. Constancy or identity in this case cannot be played off against change or variation, but the former must be included in the latter and *vice versa*.

Thus, we are led inexorably into describing the method of dialectics. In this method the unity of opposites is conceived of and explained logically and conceptually. Before continuing, it may be helpful to give a provisional definition of dialectics: generally, it is the notion that the basic principle of logic is not the principle of non-contradiction, A over against non-A, but that a more basic unity exists which includes and relativizes this opposition. This may strike one as strange and in a way it is. The whole effort of German Idealism, especially of Hegel, failed and has never again been attempted in the same manner and on the same scale. In order to avoid a too facile dismissal of this attempt, however, we must take note of two things: the pervasive impact it exercised and the similarity of fundamental motive that it has with all of modern Western thought.

2.2.   Although this curious attempt failed and was not repeated, it nevertheless impressed many intellectuals to such an extent that most modern philosophical currents can be meaningfully considered as reactions to Hegelian Idealism. Its central placement of the function of history, or more correctly, historicity (i.e., becoming or self-cultivation), has been preserved, albeit in a different form, in positivism, in pragmatism, distinctly in the so-called philosophy-of-life (Dilthey), and in existentialism. It has even permeated the more practical attitudes of life in the present. It manifests itself everywhere that man's historicity is viewed as central: it defines man as the being who is not fixed, but who is a process of historical self-realization.

It is also important to point out, in addition to the fact that most philosophical currents can be considered a reaction against Hegelian philosophy and that it has penetrated into our practical view of life, that this strange conception was born of a dual motive: to do justice to the alleged originality and pervasion of the free and mobile spirit or mind, and at the same time, to accommodate the claim of conceptual theoretical thought that it comprises or encompasses the whole of reality, including this free spirit itself. This two-fold motive as such, was not new or peculiar to Hegel. In the development of modern Western thought it has expressed itself in many variations.

2.3.   German Idealism in general was an impressive attempt to continue the transcendental critical line of Kant and, simultaneously, to surmount his precarious and sometimes troublesome dualisms. These dualisms were related to his attempt to reflect upon both the subject and, at the same time, the universally valid preconditions of knowledge. Even beforehand the enterprise might be expected to be difficult, if not impossible; for these dualisms are actually intimately related to Kant's notion of a serious and tenable critical enterprise. In Kant these two are inseparable; the dualisms could not be dismissed in order to accommodate his struggle for a critical philosophy. Nevertheless, let us examine this attempt of German Idealism a little more closely.

2.4. The German Idealists sided with Kant's Copernican revolution and its attempt to discover the real and true condition for experience in the subject. Kant's exposition of human dignity as located in the field of practical reason especially impressed them. The freedom, the self-determination of man had been brought out most explicitly in this exploration of practical reason. However, precisely because of this emphasis, German Idealists became dissatisfied with Kant's formalism and intellectualism, not only in this sphere but also in the sphere of pure theoretical reason. They wanted to do fuller justice to the human subject in its free autonomous self-determination, in its formative activity and self-realization instead of just pure intellectual forms. They tried to achieve this through the idea of an absolute mind or spirit. This mind or spirit is absolute because it produces itself and all its contents in a process of self-development. This notion of "producing", in a somewhat different sense, is also important for understanding Marxist thought.

2.5. The absolute Idealists were also dissatisfied with the independence and obscurity of the thing-in-itself, for it was really a natural thing-in-itself. They attempted to conceive of nature itself in a spiritual way, that is, as a product of the absolute mind or spirit. Dialectics served as the method by which this was to be achieved. Mind-in-itself, is so full and productive that, in order to experience and to show this productive power, it needs something *else*, in which it externalizes itself, namely nature. As such, nature is the necessary "other" of mind, and this gives it its distinctness, but this does not detract from its being – the – other – *of – mind*: it remains "owned" by mind. Even its "necessity" is a necessity in function of free production. Everything depends on mind, for even the process of distinguishing nature from mind is performed by mind itself. Mind discovers nature by way of reflection, as in a mirror: nature is discovered to be mind itself but at the same time distinguished from it. Mind discovers *what it is*, in all its possibilities, by discovering *what it is not*. The power of self-reflective activity is strong enough to stand this opposition – even, if need be, to be "permissive" with respect to 'unmindlike" phenomena –, and to include the opposition in its process of self-unfolding.

9

One of the main possibilities of mind in its self-development, is nature which appears as an obstacle, as something which resists mind. Thus, it is one of the greatest challenges to mind: a challenge on which to try out its own potentials as mind. Nature as an obstacle is necessary to mind in order to challenge it to try out the full range of its possibilities. However, this obstacle is simultaneously conceived in terms of logical opposites or contradictions, i.e., in terms of dialectics. Therefore, Idealism uses the current logical concepts and distinctions, and formulates the thesis: mind distinguishes itself from itself. As an inexhaustible source of possibilities mind is in need of some obstacle in order to be able to come to itself: but it must come to itself by becoming aware, in an experimental way, of the real fullness of its possibilities.

These Idealist problematics are a development of the problematics started in the philosophy of Kant, except that the former added some problematics of its own. Some idealists came to the general conclusion that true nature is organic nature: animated and spiritually orientated. In this connection it is interesting to note that Schelling tried to elaborate this organic and spiritually oriented view of nature in an aesthetic direction; art becomes for him the main revelation of this dialectical unity of mind and nature.

2.6. Our final point also serves as a transition to the Marxian enterprise. The whole idea and striving of German Idealism continued to be determined as a theoretical enterprise, as a striving of theoretical reflection. It is important to notice this, for it constitutes another motive, in fact, the basic driving power behind this dialectical method of thinking. Precisely because of its freedom, the mind or spirit cannot be dogmatically posited; for this dogmatic position would clash with that radical freedom. According to German Idealism, free mind only has value if it is established critically, not dogmatically, as the only possible basic principle. This is obviously part of the Kantian heritage of the critical attitude. In accordance with the whole Western philosophical tradition, the German Idealists continue to use the term "critical" to mean *"by way of theoretical reflection"*. This presupposition that true criticism comes only by way of theoretical reflection, is itself an untested dogma.

2.7. Kant had also tried to critically account for this basic position and to make possible for the knowing subject this wide scope. This attempt is found in his famous *transcendental logic*, the major part of the *Critique of Pure Reason*, where he intended to give a justification for the claims of the subject. That turned out to be a difficult part of his philosophy. But for the post-Kantian Idealists, especially Hegel, who wanted to remain both a truly scientific logical thinker and a "spiritual" thinker, the problem is even more difficult. Hegel wanted to be critically responsible by meeting the requirements of genuine and pure reflective thought, but he also wanted to satisfy the principle of free spirit as the real source and central productive power of reality as a whole. If indeed free spirit is the source of reality as a whole, then pure reflective thought itself can only be considered as the thought *of* this free spirit or mind, not primarily as thought *about* mind. Pure reflective thought must then share the main properties of the free spirit: the properties of *mobility* and *original production*. But if this is the case, how can it be considered any longer as a critical accounting for, and justification of, the central place and fundamental possibilities of mind? Hegel tried to solve these basic problematics by his dialectics. He introduced this method in order to demonstrate simultaneously the right of the subject to claim its central productive position and the right of thought itself to claim productive mobility.

2.8. This differed from Kant's method of demonstration in his transcendental logic, which retained more of the idea of logical proof than Hegel's attempt. Unless we understand this, we will not come to grips with Hegel. Hegel's attempt to solve this problematic failed; in fact, it even intensified the problem and brought it to a head. In Hegel's dialectical demonstration there is no place for a human subject or *ego* that transcends theoretical reflection. Kant tried to find a place for this subject in the field of practical reason, but post-Kantian Idealism can no longer find room for the human subject as a supra-logical identity; for in this idealist conception even the history of this subject, that is to say, its historical self-development, is grasped entirely within the framework of dialectical thought.

2.9. On the other hand, this reflective thought, although it claims to be critical, is in danger of degenerating into a means of power in the hands of free productive spirit. As such, it overwhelms, picks up and obliterates all distinctions and antitheses or oppositions within itself. The German Idealists called this process of abolition "ideal", which is to them the same as "real". In short, on the one hand, there is no longer a safe place for the human subject in its freedom, since it must be grasped in the framework of dialectical theoretical thought; and on the other hand, this very dialectical thought, critical as it claims to be, is in danger of degenerating into a means of power that cuts through all distinctions. Thus, the problematics we have been tracing apparently lead to a dilemma and are finally brought to a head. It is at this point that Marx enters the scene.

11

CHAPTER II

The Marxian Reaction to Hegel

1. *Marx's View of Nature in his Dissertation*

We can learn a great deal about Marx's intentions from the annotations to his dissertation. Marx's dissertation dealt with the philosophy of nature of Democritus and Epicurus. Aristotle occupies a historical position midway between Democritus and Epicurus. In the extant histories of ancient Greek philosophy Aristotle was seen as an end, as Hegel was seen to be for modern philosophy in the eyes of many intellectuals of Marx's day; Marx wanted to show that Aristotle was not an absolute end, but that the philosophy of nature reached a new height in the philosophy of Epicurus whom he calls the greatest "enlightener" of Greek philosophy.

1.1. Marx's choice of the philosophy of nature as a theme for his dissertation is significant. He felt, in our opinion, rightly, that nature had not received its due in German Idealism. For Kant, nature as it really is had vanished *behind* the "screen" as the unknowable thing-in-itself, while that which appeared on the "screen" was projected there by the formal *a-prioris* of the camera of consciousness. German Idealism either adopted Kant's view of nature or it viewed nature as the dialectical counterpart, but at the same time also the product, of thinking mind. Actually, the philosophy of nature was the weak point of Hegel's philosophy; for mind itself was in need of something other to stimulate its own development: nature fulfilled this requirement. However, this same nature also was discovered to be the mirror image of this pre-conceived mind itself. Thus, it is no wonder that Marx felt it necessary to come to grips with the problem of nature. Avoiding the Kantian interpretation of nature as having vanished behind the "screen" and also the post-Kantian view of nature as both a mere obstacle and a product of mind, Marx tried to account for nature in its just-being-there. He tries to give a new explanation of man's relationship to nature. However, Marx's thought is too complex to enable us to label it simply as a kind of naturalism.

Already in the conclusion of his dissertation where he judges Epicurus in relation to Democritus his thought gives evidence of this complexity:

12

he states that, "in Epicurus, the atomistic theory with all its contradictions has been elaborated as a natural science of self-consciousness".[1] Marx's reference to a natural science of self-consciousness is, of course, related to his evaluation of Epicurus as the greatest "enlightener" of the early Greeks – the "enlightener" of mind. Thus, Marx sees in Epicurus an attempt at a science of self-consciousness; whereas in Democritus the atom is nothing but the objective expression of empirical science and of nature in general. Apparently, his praise of Epicurus was based on an interpretation of him as the philosopher who took nature seriously in close relation to human self-consciousness.

2. Marx's Reinterpretation of Theory in the Annotations to his Dissertation

The most interesting and important statements in the annotations to Marx's dissertation are found in a section called, "The World Becoming Philosophical and Philosophy Becoming Worldly". Marx states that,

> It is a psychological law that the theoretical mind having become free-in-itself passes into practical energy; as *will*... it turns against the reality of the world which exists without it... The *praxis* of philosophy itself, however, is a theoretical one. That is to say, it is a critique that compares individual existence with essence, particular reality to the idea. However, this *immediate realization* of philosophy according to its inner being is affected with contradictions, and this inner being takes shape in the appearance and puts its mark upon this appearance[2].

Since discussion of what Marx has in mind when he speaks about the psychological law in this context would lead us too far away from our real topic, we shall bypass this question. For Marx, Hegelian philosophy is the culmination of all philosophy: in it the theoretical mind has unfolded its own inner and free possibilities completely. This, however, does not rule out the possibility of further development. Marx thought that this development should be in a more practical direction. This is what he means when he says, "it is a psychological law that the theoretical mind having become free-in-itself passes into practical energy".

2.1.   But what does this becoming practical of the theoretical mind mean? First, it means that there is a *continuity* in the development of the free theoretical mind as it passes over into practical energy; secondly, that this development, since it is in accordance with a psychological law, is necessary and, to a certain extent, automatic; thirdly, since something new appears in this development, there is also *discontinuity*: the theoretical mind passes over into practical energy, becomes *will*.

[1] K. Marx, Frühe Schriften, ed. by H.-J. Lieber and P. Furth, Stuttgart 1962, p. 69 (translation by author).
[2] K. Marx, o.c., p. 71 (translation by author).

Already here, the situation appears to be dialectical, for continuity and discontinuity exist at the same time. Philosophy, i.e., theoretical mind, continues to be philosophy, but it has a new position or function; as *praxis*, it becomes *will* or as Marx puts it here: "immediate realization". This situation can be described as dialectical because it is shot through with contradiction. Because philosophy itself is here at stake as a theoretical enterprise working with logical means, Marx felt it necessary to interpret it in terms of *logical* contradiction. But, at the same time, philosophy is a historical enterprise that needs to be developed; thus, this continuity and discontinuity, this profound dialectic, not only affects the methods used by philosophy, but the situation of philosophy itself. Marx points this out when he refers to these contradictions as affecting the "realization of philosophy according to its inner being".

2.2. However, there is a basic problem in this argument which is not brought out by Marx. On the one hand, Marx sticks to a theoretical mind (philosophy) as an independent and separate entity that just happens to be there and which reaches its culmination in Hegelian philosophy. Even when he goes on to speak of the necessity of a further development, this remains a development of philosophical theoretical mind which is assumed to exist as an independent entity. When he introduces *will*, the practical energy, these remain theoretically determined factors. Yet, something new has to happen; for theoretical mind passes into practical energy and reveals itself as *will*, (or as *will to power*, to use an expression of Nietzsche). This will encounters the resistant reality of the world as it is in-itself and turns against this world that exists without it. A conflict is, thus, inevitable; consequently, any further development *has to be* a revolutionary development, although Marx does not explicitly use the word "revolutionary" here. The psychological law that we took note of above determines this development. But even if we leave it out of consideration, a problem remains: for we must not forget that all of Marx's discussion still pivots on that preconceived idea of a theoretical mind in its autonomous development.

2.3. At this point we must ask how these apparently contradictory notions can be united or made compatible. We have, on the one hand, a supposedly independent entity named theoretical mind which must be retained in its continuous development, and, on the other hand, a radical change in which this mind passes over into *will* and becomes critical in its clash with the existing world. If they cannot be united or made compatible, is it still possible to interpret this situation in terms of logical contradiction? [This question is closely related to another question which we will develop later on, namely, whether this logical contradiction is "interior", i.e. belongs to the inner essence of

14

philosophical thought itself, or whether it is discovered by thought as existing in the "outer", the resistant world?]

2.4.   Certain elements in the above quoted passage cause us to recall Kant. Marx, like Kant, insists here on the necessity for being critical; he also invokes the Kantian theme of the relationship between theoretical and practical reason. Therefore, it might be instructive to speculate what Kant would have said with regard to Marx's formulation of the problem. In our fictional dialogue Kant would have said that these two things cannot be united; for when Marx posits his notion of the practical energy of the theoretical mind or when he explains his idea of critique as being philosophical theory in practice ("the *praxis* of philosophy itself, however, is a theoretical one"), Kant would have replied that this problematic demonstrates the impossibility of trying to surmount duality by means of a totalitarian enterprise, which is the folly that all post-Kantian Idealism falls into with disastrous results. For from the viewpoint of Kant, what Marx is doing here is confusing pure theoretical reason and practical reason, as well as their different fields. This confusion would have been a clear sign to Kant of the lack of both a truly critical sense and critical reflection; for truly critical reflection requires this very duality of pure theoretical reason and practical reason in order to preserve the purity of scientific knowledge in its universal validity as well as moral freedom and moral responsibility. However, we do not mean to present Kant's position as normative; for, as we have observed, his position, too, was full of unsolved problems and embarrassing tensions that called for resolution. Thus, we see the remarkable ambiguity inherent in the use of such important notions as critical, practical and theoretical by both Kant and Marx. These notions can not be taken for granted or at face value in the works of even the greatest philosophers, for they display a similar ambiguity almost everywhere. We must always subject them to an analysis of how they actually function in the whole of the philosophical argument.

3. *The Ambiguity of Marx's Breakthrough of Theory*

3.1.   In a certain sense, Marx does not want to maintain that this contradiction can be resolved either; he says that when the theoretical mind turns into *will* (practical energy), we meet with contradictions. At first sight this view seems very similar to Kant. However, this assertion does not prevent Marx from reducing these contradictions to and explaining them in terms of the very nature of theoretical mind itself and the necessity of its development. The very term, *contradiction*, testifies to the absolute position that a theoretical mind maintains in Marx's thought; for it is a theoretical, logical term. This impossible situation can only be somewhat clarified when we assume

15

that the notion of the *will to power* has been present all the time. If we assume that the *will to power* has been present as the motivating force behind this theoretical philosophical mind, which seems to be Marx's absolute starting point, we can begin to understand Marx a little better, although his position still appears impossible. This *will to power*, present from the beginning, first tried to realize itself within the theoretical enterprise; but it became obvious to Marx that it had to break through the limitations of this theoretical enterprise in order to become full-fledged *will*, because its demands could no longer be satisfied within these theoretical limitations. Although this assumption makes it easier to understand Marx, nevertheless certain questions remain. First, although Marx speaks of a breakthrough of the limitations of theoretical thought, has he actually achieved a real breakthrough? Secondly, although we spoke of Marx's awareness of the necessity of this breakthrough, what do we mean by this awareness, i.e., was he aware of the full depth of the necessity?

The first question is whether a real breakthrough exists if the theoretical mind remains the starting point that determines, to a certain extent, its relation to the world. It is true that Marx says the world is there as real and resistant, but he continually posits this world as an object, that is to say, as a theoretical object – *Gegenstand* – of the theoretical mind. His attempt at explaining all the conflicts and oppositions in the world in terms of contradictions, as Hegel had done before him, testifies to the same tendency. We cannot speak of a real breakthrough of the *will*, for which Marx was seeking, because it remains checked by this preconceived theoretical mind. Actually, his argument is an indication of a real crisis in philosophy and of the turning point of the nineteenth century. This crisis pertains also to the critique that Marx presents as a proper *praxis* of theoretical philosophy. We cannot understand Marx unless we recognize this crisis of philosophy and the need for a real breakthrough.

The second question concerns how and in what sense the necessity of a breakthrough became evident to Marx. Although Marx's search is partly theoretical – recall the problematic position of the concept of nature in Hegelian philosophy – it is primarily undertaken at a pre-theoretical level. Marx was moved by the remaining and newly arisen needs, conflicts and oppositions of this real world, which had not been abolished despite the totalitarian claims of Hegel's system. Marx thought that these needs and conflicts, which continue to exist and to resist such totalitarian claim, ought to be abolished *will*fully in a supra-theoretical way. Without being aware of this dual motive of Marx in his theoretical starting point and in his experienced need for a breakthough, we cannot fully understand either his doctrines or his intentions.

16

3.2. The import of the annotations to Marx's dissertation is the crisis that they signalize in the philosophical conception of critique that he had mentioned as the proper *praxis* of theoretical philosophy. Although a breakthrough was clearly necessary, there was also an unsolved problem which had not yet been brought out even by Marx, namely, the problem of the limits and the possibility of that breakthrough when the starting point remains this same independent theoretical mind. The theoretical mind as *will* had to undergo a real change while at the same time remaining the same preconceived theoretical mind in its abstract nature. Marx seems to refer to just this problem when he remarks that the *praxis* of philosophy remains a theoretical one and then goes on to say that contradictions are connected with this immediate realization of philosophy: Philosophy, which becomes a critique, is the immediate realization of philosophy, and conversely, the immediate realization of philosophy means that it must become a critique. It is this that involves contradictions, according to Marx.

3.3. One of the contradictions that becomes apparent in Marx's notion of the realization, the becoming worldly of philosophy, is that philosophy encounters a world that happens to be there and which presents itself – a world which can therefore not be assimilated or included in this philosophy. This contradiction is pointed out by Marx himself.

In this particular context Marx does not clarify what he means by "worldly". One of the main features of the world in Marx's sense is that it is characterized by having a certain structure which happens to be there. This agrees with the whole context of how Marx speaks about the world in the annotations to his dissertation. In one sense, it can be called a material substructure, but it is not merely a material substructure; for Marx never fully isolates this material substructure from man's being active, being productive in and with this substructure. Man in the history of his productivity and activity makes certain discoveries and inventions that determine, to a certain extent, the productive situation in which he finds himself; but at the same time (and here things get complicated), that world, including man in his productivity, is also a product of productive mankind. Thus, although Marx keeps repeating that the world just happens to be there, this no longer appears to be obvious.

The world's being-there for Marx does not mean the same thing as the thing-in-itself in Kant's philosophy. For, although Kant's conception was oriented to a view of nature, it is a nature conceived of as a complex of substances which have several different modes of appearance. Moreover, to Kant our knowledge is only a knowledge of phenomena, and although he ultimately had to posit a thing-in-itself, he never did much with it. However, insofar as Kant maintains the concept of

17

a thing-in-itself, he cannot be said to agree with the Marxist notion of a world that happens to be there.

3.4. In fact, Marx acknowledges and even points out a further contradiction: philosophy itself is a closed totalitarian system that changes profoundly. The first contradiction that we raised arises in the immediate realization of philosophy, in its becoming worldly, when it encounters a world that happens to be there, a world that presents itself. However, this is a sort of philosophical encounter, since this conflict appears in the process of the realization of philosophy. Whereas, in this second contradiction a profound change takes place in philosophy itself: it can no longer remain a closed totalitarian system. This is specifically brought out in Marx's subsequent argument:

> As this philosophy turns outside against the appearing world, as will, the system has degraded to an abstract totality. That is to day, it has become one side of the world over against which another side stands... Inspired by the drive to realize itself, it gets in tension with something else. The inner self-sufficiency and its being rounded off [in other words, the closed character of philosophy] has been broken. That which was inner life becomes a consuming flame turning outwards. Consequently, the world becoming philosophical is at the same time philosophy becoming worldly; the realization of philosophy is at the same time its loss; that which it fights against is at the same time its own inner lack [deficiency][3].

Here the theme, "the world becoming philosophical" and "philosophy becoming worldly", appears explicitly. This passage also points to the crisis in philosophical thought produced by its having to face up to the urgent reality of the world.

However, we now return to the question whether Marx himself did not raise the problem we mentioned previously, namely, the problem of the limits and the possibility of that breakthrough when the starting point remains that same independent theoretical mind. The above passage, especially, gives the impression that the problem has been adequately raised. But we must not forget, first of all, that what Marx is saying in this quotation holds for him only after, and because of, the inner consummation of philosophical thought as such, namely, in Hegel. This remains a presupposition for Marx. In the second place, although Marx's proclamation of a new stage, announcing a reality that exists in its own right and urgency, is again brought to the fore (over against absolute idealism), we must not forget that it remains primarily a reality-in-relation, more specifically, a reality in oppositional relation to a priorly posited philosophical thought. Thirdly, in spite of what Marx says in the above-quoted passage about the degradation of philosophy as system by the emphasis on critique, this detracts little or nothing from what we have just said.

³ K. Marx, o.c., p. 71/72.

Unfortunately, Marx somewhat simplistically plays off philosophy as system and philosophy as critique over against each other. The inner connection between the systematic feature and the critical feature of authentic philosophical thought deserves a more adequate presentation. This is a complicated procedure that involves more than a mere playing off of one against the other, and fortunately so, otherwise philosophical systematics would be building castles in the sky, which may perhaps be impressive, but which would lead to the degeneration of philosophical critique into a collection of demagogical and agitative slogans. The inner connection between system and critique is necessary. However, this false opposition between the two persists as an important factor in the further development of Marxism.

4. *Marcuse's Struggle with Theory* (Excursion)

At this point we make a sudden jump to the present in order to show how this false opposition is still present today in someone like Marcuse, despite the fact that he tries to consider the relationship anew. This is especially obvious in his essay, "Philosophy and Critical Theory", in the collection entitled *Negations*. Here Marcuse argues that the traditional system-building of philosophy is no longer of any use. This is because reason (by which he means about the same thing as Marx meant by "theoretical mind") has to become a penetrating critical theory of society. Insofar as he aims at those impressive but highly abstract speculations and constructions of a so-called pure reason (that preconceived theoretical mind), he has a point; but insofar as he sets up a general contrast which posits a general opposition between philosophy and critical theory of society, he displays a reactionary attitude. And, like all reactions, it remains too much determined by that which it is reacting against. That is to say, on the one hand, it remains too strongly attached to that traditional idea of an abstract philosophical construction as the product of a preconceived autonomous theoretical mind, and on the other hand, it contrives false alternatives.

4.1. In clarifying what we mean by the latter (false alternatives), we must point out that Marcuse does not hesitate to call the measures, or the standards and the regulative ideas of his critical theory, utopian. He states that,

> Like philosophy, it [critical theory] opposes making reality into a criterion in the manner of complacent positivism. But unlike philosophy, it always derives its goals only from present tendencies of the social process. Therefore it has no fear of the utopia that the new order is denounced as being. When truth cannot be realized within the established social order, it always appears to the latter as mere utopia. This transcendence speaks not against, but for, its truth[4].

[4] H. Marcuse, *Negations*, p. 143.

This critical turn of theory no longer pertains to reality as it is; it can no longer account for the relevance of its standards to reality; thus, it is indeed utopian. One could object that surely the matter is somewhat more complicated than that: for Marcuse says that, in the first place, this critical theory "always derives its goals only from the present tendencies of the social process". This appears to be clear evidence of an attempt on his part to be realistic, in a sense. In the second place, he claims that there is only an apparent utopianism in his thought, i.e., his critical theory only *seems* to be utopian to the *established* social order. Thus, it must be admitted that his arguments do not leave him open to the charge of a simple utopianism; things are indeed somewhat more complicated.

4.2.   But does he avoid our charge of utopianism completely? There does not seem to be a sufficient basis for any inferences with regard to utopianism, or even with regard to a semblance of utopianism. Marcuse's statement that goals are derived from the present tendencies of the social process as it really is, as it really occurs, could even be interpreted in a positivistic, or a pragmatistic, or even in a more opportunistic sense. One's interpretation of this remark depends on his view of these present tendencies and their relationship to past and future tendencies: on one's view of the force, impact, meaning, constancy and distinctness of these present tendencies in the whole context of the historical process. In fact, it could even be interpreted in a more or less fatalistic sense: if one were to adopt a basic dependence upon these tendencies, he would be led to a certain passivity, for he would not really require any inferential statement of goals at all. But Marcuse does want to speak of goals, in which case, one has to suppose that these present tendencies bring about these goals from their own resources, out of their own inexorable force. Of course, this fatalistic interpretation is not at all what Marcuse intends. Nevertheless, it seems that Marcuse's thought suffers from a fundamental polarity and vacillation between an extreme activism and a dash of passive resignation. What is remarkable is that the interpretations of this particular clause (the goals being derived from present tendencies of the social process), whether they be more positivistic or more fatalistic, are all different manifestations of a fundamental historicism.[5]

As a matter of fact, this historicism is not only active in Marcuse, but also in quite a few discussions of Christians. Many Christians feel that they are standing at the parting of two contemporary and seemingly all-important paths: that of conservatism and of progressivism. They

[5] In defining historicism, we can well make use of Marcuse's notion of deriving goals from present tendencies in the social process (by which he also means the historical process): every attempt to derive ultimate goals from present or even past historical tendencies may be called historicism.

seem to think of this crossroad as an inevitable and basic dilemma. However, this merely testifies to their being affected by the same historicism. Thus, there is no need or reason for Christians to look down on Marcuse with his polarities and vacillations; nevertheless, this should not prevent us from trying to maintain our critical balance, also in relation to his conceptions. His derivation of goals from the present tendencies of the social process as such does not imply the need to introduce the term utopia. The other possible interpretations that we gave of this clause demonstrate that the use of the term utopia is unwarranted; for it can be interpreted in certain realistic senses that can hardly be labelled utopian.

4.3.   At this point, we must add a second comment with regard to the first possible objection that we raised above, namely, that Marcuse's position is more complicated than just criticism passing over into simple utopianism. This finds support in Marcuse's constant appeal to the social process in its *real* development. Note that in our preceding argument we quoted Marcuse but added, to the phrase "the social process", *as it really is.* We did so in order to bring out what we believe is his intention. Without this addition, there would appear to be no clear difference between his critical theory and philosophy with its ideal constructions. In order to clarify what is involved here, we must ask: what does this appeal to the social process itself really mean? For when Marcuse appeals to the social process, his conception already contains a profound ambiguity within itself. Although it is not obvious from this passage,[6] Marcuse conceives of it as a dialectical process, in the sense that potentiality is always and necessarily at variance with actuality, actuality being the establishment in the broadest sense and at a given moment. With regard to the main point of our discussion, the consequences of this notion depend on whether one sees the dialectical character of the social process *mainly* as a clear and strict law that universally determines historical events, or whether one places the *main emphasis* upon dialectics as a flexible means employed by a subjective power in the struggle to make history. Note that "mainly" or "main emphasis" is underscored because usually neither of these possibilities appears in its pure form.

In the first case, if dialectics is conceived of as a strict law, there is hardly any reason for introducing utopia or utopian, for then determinism would be a more obvious option, since dialectics then functions as a clear and strict law that determines historical events universally. Although this determinism may take different forms, it nevertheless, in the final analysis, remains a determinism.

Nor is it necessary to introduce utopian elements in the second case.

[6] See for example his *One-dimensional Man*, p. 171 ff.

For if the main emphasis is on dialectics as a flexible means employed by subjective power, then dialectics is little more than an expression of the resolute will of a certain historical subject to revolt actively against a certain actual situation.

When Marcuse speaks of utopia with regard to the derivation of goals from the present tendencies of the dialectical process, he apparently has in mind the social process itself, but seen in the light of certain preconceived utopian ideas and standards. At the same time, he uses the term "social process" to signify his concern with and about reality. This is precisely the profound ambiguity already mentioned with regard to the use of the term "social process" itself. This concludes our remarks concerning the first possible objection.

4.4. Returning to the second possible objection, the objection that Marcuse's utopianism is only apparent because his view only seems to be utopian to the established social order, we must admit to its validity, although it detracts somewhat from our main point. However, it should be clarified by two remarks. Initially, at least, this semblance of utopianism is inevitable within and to the established and existing social order; thus, this critical theory confesses that it is unable to persuade the establishment or existing social order. Accordingly, it is irrelevant to that order, at least, in the sense of being unable to persuade it; thus, it is, in a sense, out of order.

Coming to the second and main counter-argument, the semblance of utopianism is not only inevitable, but it is also and primarily a necessary semblance. Because of the basic polarity between potentiality and actuality that we referred to earlier, the existing social order is not simply an accidental situation – a result of certain contingent circumstances which as such are alien to the social process to which Marcuse appeals. It is rather one of the realizations or actualizations of a certain potentiality: thus, it can be called a real potentiality of dialectical history (or social process) itself. Since it is not just an accidental matter alien to the social process as a whole, it is a realization of a real potentiality; thus, it is, in a sense, ultimate, because it cannot be subjected to a certain higher, supra-historical standard. True, it will have to be replaced because of the dialectical law which requires that every establishment has to be replaced by new possibilities, by a new potential order. However, this established situation, this existing social order can neither be ignored nor even condemned, because a condemnation would imply an appeal to certain standards beyond the socio-historical process. This Marcuse cannot allow. We have here discovered why Marcuse needs a transcendent or, as he calls it in the passage quoted above, a "transcendence" by means of utopia.

4.5. To this point we have been trying to explain the reactionary attitude of Marcuse. We called attention to the fact that he contrives

22

false alternatives and in this context we discussed the problems and inconsistencies of his conception of utopia. But just previously we mentioned another feature of Marcuse's reactionary attitude, namely, his permanent attachment to the traditional ideal of abstract philosophy – philosophy as a product of an abstract, preconceived theoretical mind. We read in the same essay in *Negations*:

> The transformation of a given status is not, of course, the business of philosophy... Adhering to the abstractness of philosophy is more appropriate to circumstances and closer to truth than is the pseudophilosophical concreteness that condescends to social struggles. What is true in philosophical concepts was arrived at by abstracting from the concrete status of man and is true only in such abstraction. Reason, mind, morality, knowledge, and happiness are not only categories of bourgeois philosophy, but concerns of mankind[7].

This quote makes it rather clear that Marcuse holds to the truth of certain abstract constructions of a preconceived, independent theoretical mind; consequently, even the utopian ideals are in turn presented in terms of abstract constructions. Further in the same essay we read:

> Its [critical theory's] constructive concepts, too, have a residue of abstractness as long as the reality toward which they are directed is not yet given. Here, however, abstractness results not from avoiding the status quo, but from orientation toward the future status of man. It cannot be supplanted by another, correct theory of the established order (as idealist abstractness was replaced by the critique of political economy). It cannot be succeeded by a new theory, but only by rational reality itself[8].

Here we observe a final attempt to identify thought and reality. In this connection we may remember that the main contention of Hegel's philosophy was also an attempt to identify thought and reality by means of dialectic.

The purpose of these quotations from Marcuse was, first, to further support our characterization of Marcuse's attitude as reactionary, namely, that he remains permanently attached to that old, traditional idea of philosophy as the independent product of an autonomous theoretical mind. In addition, incredible as it may seem, we have even observed Marcuse attempting, in the tradition of Hegel, to identify thought and reality, albeit "eschatologically".

In this chapter we have dealt with statements made by Marx early in his dissertation. The main point we tried to make regards the polarity inherent in Marx's view respecting philosophy as system and of philosophy as critique. We went on to examine Marcuse's reconsideration of that relationship and polarity. It became clear that this profound polarity persists also in his thought and that he has not been able to break with the stratagem of playing off system over against critique.

---

[7] H. Marcuse, *Negations*, p. 147.
[8] *Negations*, pp. 153, 154.

CHAPTER III

Marx's debt to Hegel

First we should clarify why, in his confrontation with Hegel, Marx concentrated especially on Hegel's philosophy of right. Marx was initially very impressed, even saturated by Hegelian philosophy. This was obvious from the annotations to his dissertation. In this dissertation, as the title shows, Marx dealt with the philosophy of nature. As a matter of fact, this was one of the weakest points in Hegel's philosophy. But Marx was really only leading up to a critical confrontation with Hegel's philosophy of right. Marx's major concern was man in his societal relationships, and in the philosophy of right Hegel gave his account of man in society. Moreover, Marx thought this to be the most fascinating and challenging part of Hegel's philosophy.

0.1. However, in order to be able to appreciate Marx's contribution, we should first prepare ourselves by briefly looking back at Hegel's philosophy. Hegel distinguished three main structures within society as a whole: first, the family, which is called the natural or immediate unity; secondly, bourgeois or civil society; and thirdly, the state, which was seen by Hegel as a morally or ethically qualified whole, the perfect form of the moral idea. According to Hegel, the state is the final, the uppermost structure of society as a whole, because certain negative moments, moments of human alienation, which have come to the fore in civil or bourgeois society have been abolished and superseded (*aufgehoben*) in the higher level of the state. We shall merely list two symptoms of human alienation that Hegel observed in civil society, and elaborate on them later. First, in civil society the natural immediacy, or one might say, the primacy of the family has been broken. It is no longer sufficient for a person to be a member of just a family, but he has to become a member of civil society as well. This is the first symptom of a kind of negativity. Secondly, instead of being a real community, civil society consists of men with an individualistic attitude towards one another.

0.2. Hegel points out a certain opposition or negativity which functions positively as a "motor" that drives each structure along the road to further development. We shall not explain how Hegel elaborates this at each level, because we wish to focus on the second structure – civil society – which is the most important one in our discussion of Marx's interpretation.

The negativity which Hegel saw in that second structure, civil society, is also the most pronounced one. It is, in a sense, the most negative structure; for Hegel looks upon it more as a necessary evil than as a positive "motor" to further development. In order to understand this, we have to take into account that Hegel as well as Marx recognized a drastic process of change in society (using the term "society" in the narrower sense: as the complex of organized labor, economic relationships, educational institutions and the like; not in the broader sense that encompasses all these structures together). According to Hegel, this process of drastic change had to find its ultimate goal and destination in the state, since the latter is the highest structure. In fact, this process demands that civil society be elevated to the higher level of the political structure, for this is the only possible way that its negativity can be eliminated. To Marx, however, this construction is unsatisfactory: the elevation of societal relationships to the higher level of the political structure is too simplistic; and, to state it rather unphilosophically, Marx was sick and tired of all that idealistic, abstract, unworldly moral stuff. Ultimately, he requires a radical reversal of these societal relationships themselves.

But, why did Marx react so vehemently against Hegel's conception and why did he consider it important to react against it? When Hegel said that the ultimate goal and destination of that drastic change in societal relationships had to be its elevation into the new structure of the state, then we must conclude that at this level these relationships become inviolable. Thus, the possibility for a radical reversal of those societal relationships themselves had been headed off by Hegel. In order to clarify this somewhat, we should first ask what Hegel conceived the main features of bourgeois society to be.

0.3.   The term "bourgeois" is already interesting in itself. It is a translation of the German term *"bürgerliche Gesellschaft"*, which although used by Hegel was not original with him, for it had been introduced previously in England and France. We have vacillated between using "civil" or "bourgeois"; however, the term "bourgeois" is actually the better translation because it conveys the mental attitude that Hegel wished to express in the term *"bürgerlich"*, namely, that of antipathy. Thus, his emphasis upon the negativity, the necessary evil of this structure appears in the very term he uses to name it. This is rather remarkable, since in the French "bourgeois" originally meant civil, which designates the characteristic of the citizen. So it originally belonged to the political sphere of the state. We have only to recall the

French Revolution in which the term "citizen" was a word to conjure with. This was thanks to Jean Jacques Rousseau.

0.4.   According to Rousseau, civil liberty, i.e., the liberty of the citizen in the state, is the most important, the highest form of liberty. We must add, however, that even Rousseau preserved another kind of liberty, figuratively speaking, in the basement of his structure: he called this man's natural liberty. This feature is important to take note of because it brings out one of the main characteristics of western political thought. This natural liberty, which is the liberty of the separate individual, is a threat to civil liberty. It threatens to introduce a kind of anarchy, and is, to that extent, potentially destructive; accordingly, it must be relegated to the basement of Rousseau's finished structure. For this reason, it also had to be superseded and elevated to the higher level – that of civil liberty. However, Rousseau could not just dismiss the natural liberty of the separate individual, so he preserves it with its own positive right, albeit only in the basement.

0.5.   Although the term "bourgeois" originally belonged to the sphere of the state, its meaning shifted to designate society, or societal relationships, in the narrower sense. The history of this word is both instructive and significant. Originally the word "civil" or "bourgeois" was used in contrast with the feudal period; the word marked the discovery of the equality of all men as individuals in the constitutional, political sense, i.e., as citizens. The structures of feudal society did not allow for the equality of all men in this sense: too many were dependent upon too few. With the discovery of this kind of equality, the opportunity for the development of society as a whole increased proportionately. However, soon this discovery began increasingly to mean: everyone for himself and God for all. Practically, this came to mean that society was dominated by interests and the collision of these interests. This practice, in turn, induced a certain mental attitude. This brings us back to an earlier point, namely, the mental attitude expressed in the term "bourgeois". The term "bourgeois" characterizes the man who is mindful of his own or his family's interests, who is striving to "feather his own nest", who is conscious of the desire to be "civilized" in a general and diluted sense. At the same time, this man falls short of a truly moral attitude towards his fellow man. This was what Hegel had noticed and, accordingly, wished to connote in his term *"bürgerlich"*; this hidden criticism also passed into the word "bourgeois". It is Hegel's desire to restore this bourgeois man who fails in his moral attitude towards his fellow man and thereby to re-establish moral contact within the state. We have thus seen how the overtones of the word "bourgeois" shifted from positive to negative, in Hegel.

0.6.   We now move on to elaborate on Hegel's understanding of bourgeois society. Hegel stresses that the main feature of bourgeois

26

society is its being founded in drives or urges and in the materialistic relationships resulting from these drives. Marx joins with Hegel on this point. Marx's criticism of Hegel is directed not so much at the analysis he gave of bourgeois society, but primarily to the fact that this society is philosophically conceived of as an intermediate stage on the way to the final destination – the state as the highest form of the moral idea. In the latter conception, Marx points out, the material relationships of life and also the possibility for improving these material relationships are idealized beforehand. For, since bourgeois society is destined to be abolished and superseded by the state, the impetus to improve material relationships has been removed.

0.7. Closely connected to this criticism, is Marx's objection to Hegel's idea of a fundamental separation between civil society and the state – a separation which was to be abolished only by society being absorbed into the state. Hegel is right, says Marx, insofar as the essence of the modern state is concerned; but Hegel is wrong in supposing that this is the way it ought to be. Marx himself advocates a more direct and more intimate connection between civil society and the state. He criticizes Hegel for neglecting the economic basis of the state itself. It is the separation resulting from this neglect that, philosophically speaking, subverts the possibility for active and concrete intervention in the material economic relationships themselves in the attempt to humanize them. With Hegel this humanization is possible only by turning to the state.

0.8. The final step Hegel took was the personification of the state in the monarch. He reasoned that since the state was a morally qualified structure, and since morality can only be derived from personhood, an institution as such being incapable of either morality or immorality, therefore, the state has to be personified in the sovereign monarch. The person of the monarch thus represents the whole moral structure. In opposition to this conception of Hegel, Marx asserts in his early writings that democracy is the essence of all political constitutions; democracy is man socialized.

Without elaborating, we wish to join with Marx's criticism of Hegel, specifically with regard to his observations on the divergence between civil society and the state: they cannot but be interrelated; a fundamental separation between them is impossible. In his later writings, however, Marx gave a peculiar interpretation of the way these two were to be interconnected: in the effort at reforming and humanizing societal relationships, he deemed it valid to make direct use of the means that belongs to the sphere of political power. With this we take issue.

0.9. So far we have discussed bourgeois society in terms of being founded in drives and in material relationships and interests. We now wish to examine another feature of bourgeois society closely related to this one. According to Hegel, bourgeois or civil society is a system of all-around interdependence; in this it displays an outward similarity to the state, which is also such a system. However, it is precisely in the outwardness of this similarity that it remains alien to the inner essence of the state. Hegel sees bourgeois society as dominated by a tendency toward need-satisfaction. Herein we find a connection with the first feature: for these needs are stimulated by the urges that were described there. This implies an outward directedness. As a member of bourgeois society, one says, "I am in need of something outside of myself". This concept of need as implying that there is something outside of oneself to which he is directed in this very need, is a rather simple interpretation. Nevertheless, in this way, a system of mutual interdependence is developed; for every individual is in need of something outside of himself. But since these needs are also rooted both in subjective desires or lusts and in a subjective arbitrariness in the striving toward the satisfaction of these desires, the system of mutual interdependence is at the same time a system dominated by the notions of "use", "profit", and "selfishness". Here again Marx sides with Hegel, as is evident from his words:

> Practical need, egoism, is the principle of civil society, and is revealed as such in its pure form as soon as civil society has fully engendered the political state. The god of practical need and self-interest is money[1].

This quotation appears in the context of a discussion on the Jewish question, in which Marx attempts to discover what characteristics of modern society the Jew embodies. The clause we wish to underscore is his thesis that "practical need, egoism, is the principle of civil society". Again we quote Marx from the same essay:

> It is because the essence of the Jew was universally realized and secularized in civil society, that civil society could not convince the Jew of the unreality of his religious essence, which is precisely the ideal representation of practical need[2].

Marx's concept of the religious essence of the Jew in modern society, as being the "ideal representation of practical need", leads to the conclusion:

> As soon as society succeeds in abolishing the empirical essence of Judaism – huckstering and its conditions – the Jew becomes impossible, because his consciousness no longer has an object. The subjective basis of Judaism – practical need – assumes a human form, and the conflict between the individual, sensuous existence of man and his species-existence is abolished.

[1] T. B. Bottomore, Karl Marx Early Writings, p. 37.
[2] Ibid., p. 40.

> The *social* emancipation of the Jew is the *emancipation of society from Judaism*[3].

So we see that Marx's contention is that the Jew is a characteristic product of civil society. The empirical essence of this society is the occasion for being a Jew. The phrase, "assumes a human form" refers to the humanization of the material relationships that are embodied in the Jew. In order to show how closely Marx follows Hegel in his characterization of society, we quote a short passage from the latter: "In civil society everybody is his own purpose and everything else is nothing to him; however, as this purpose cannot be realized without relationships to other people, these other people are means to the aim [the purpose] of the particular individual",[4] that is to say, the aim of being one's own aim, of being one's own purpose.

0.10. Having discussed how civil society is founded in drives or urges, and having pointed out that it displays an all-around interdependence, we now come to the third and final feature of civil or bourgeois society, namely, that it is, in a certain sense, unlimited. This is closely related to the features we have already discussed: the unceasing urges toward need-satisfaction lead to an unlimited selfishness. As a result, in bourgeois society there exists no primary limiting relation that governs relationships between people. An animal, says Hegel, has limited needs, but man can extend his needs indefinitely, if only by enumerating and detailing them, which can be an infinite process. In the *Philosophy of Right* Hegel says, "Every convenience (or comfort) shows its inconvenience (or discomfort) and those inventions are endless".[5] In other words, man liberates himself from the pressure of immediate natural necessity; however, in comparison with the animal, he subjects himself to new necessities which he produces himself. Thus, Hegel showed that man can artificially create needs which are actually not real needs. Marx also adopted this interpretation.

Thus, Hegel sketches a picture of civil society as an anonymous, formidable power. It is a system in which the total mutual interdependence of everyone on everyone is founded on a universal selfishness. As Hegel once put it, "Slaves [also in the economic sense of the term] need the master, but the master could not be a master without the slave". What Hegel means to say here is that the self, in a dialectical sense, coincides with the mutual dependence of all the people on each other. This situation is radically opposed to real self-development and self-realization. For the latter can only take place when people see themselves as members of an organic whole. Of course, this is precisely

[3] Bottomore, p. 40.
[4] *Hegels Sämtliche Werke*, ed. Glockner, vol. 7, p. 263.
[5] *Ibid.*, p. 273.

what civil society is not. Thus, says Hegel, the dialectic of civil society is an almost disintegrating dialectic. However, Hegel's observation to this effect carries a somewhat less serious import than when Marx makes the same observation. For Marx maintains that the only solution to this thoroughly negative situation is a catastrophic one. Whereas, for Hegel, civil society is an intermediate stage in the development of the state; a final solution at a higher level – that of the moral idea – is inevitable. However, even for Hegel the state does display some traces of the disintegrative negativity of the preceding stage of civil society. The moral character of the state does not mean that it is just a mild, friendly father; because of the remaining traces of negativity, it must also be a power organization, which at times has to impose its will by force. According to Hegel, even wars are sometimes necessary.

It would be interesting to examine Hegel's conception of civil society further, but the above points are adequate to make clear Marx's ties to Hegel. As a matter of fact, our exposition not only served to prepare us for a better understanding of Marx's contribution to a critique of Hegel's philosophy of right (the points treated not all being immediately relevant to this topic), but it also served to prepare us for a better understanding of Marx's other earlier works. We now turn to the essay our remarks have been leading up to: *Contribution to the Critique of Hegel's Philosophy of Right*.

CHAPTER IV

Marx's "Contribution to the critique of Hegel's Philosophy of Right"

1. *Introduction*

The heart of this essay can be found in two sentences: "In short, *you cannot abolish philosophy without realizing it.*"[1] "Its principal defect may be summarized as follows: *it believed that it could realize philosophy without abolishing it.*"[2] The latter position was maintained by a certain political party in the Germany of Marx's day. In response to that position Marx makes these two complementary assertions: you cannot abolish philosophy without realizing it; and it is impossible to realize philosophy without abolishing it. Note the continuity between these remarks and the annotations to his dissertation. The main theme of the annotations was philosophy becoming worldly and the world becoming philosophical. Marx then went on to discuss the contradictions inherent in this dual process. We pointed out the presence of the free theoretical mind which had to undergo a change in becoming practical and in becoming a critique. We also pointed out that what Marx was dealing with was a crisis in philosophy itself, that although he was dealing with the necessity of a breakthrough outward, it nevertheless remained a breakthrough of philosophy as such. Marx agreed with Hegel in this respect. We also noted a more profound affinity between Marx and Hegel in this context. For Hegel, too, theoretical mind or philosophy as such had to incorporate a practical will to power. This was the ultimate motive underlying the dialectical method, which is an attempt to break through the limitations of the logical principles of identity and contradiction by logical means. Thus, dialectic turned out to be a practical means of power that served to express the comprehensiveness of the free (will-full) absolute spirit within a framework that appeared to remain theoretical. A strange combination indeed! Nevertheless, the most profound affinity between Marx and Hegel was to be found at precisely this point. However, in grappling with the urgency and resistance of the factual questions and problems that

---

[1] T. B. Bottomore, *Karl Marx Early Writings*, p. 50. All quotes are from this edition unless otherwise indicated.
[2] *Ibid.*, p. 51.

31

persisted in reality, Marx was struck by the largely imaginary character of Hegel's so-called final solution, especially because Hegel claimed that his was a total solution.

This summary was meant to accentuate the real issues and also the real limitations of Marx's struggle. These are epitomized in the two sentences that we quoted above and called the heart of the essay. But the full content and purpose of these sentences can only become clear through a careful study of Marx's argument in the essay. But before we do this, we must first explore two main points by way of providing background: first, Marx's critique of religion; and secondly, the contemporary German situation as seen by Marx.

2. *Marx's Critique of Religion*

In order to begin our examination of Marx's critique of religion, we quote the opening paragraphs of Marx's "Contribution to the Critique of Hegel's Philosophy of Right" which serve as an introduction to the essay:

> For Germany, the *critique of religion* has been largely completed; and the criticism of religion is the premise of all criticism.
>
> The *profane* existence of error is compromised once its *celestial oratio pro aris et focis* has been refuted. Man, who has found in the fantastic reality of heaven, where he sought a supernatural being, only his own reflection, will no longer be tempted to find only the *semblance* of himself – a non-human being – where he seeks and must seek his true reality.
>
> The basis of irreligious criticism is this: *man makes religion*; religion does not make man. Religion is indeed man's self-consciousness and self-awareness so long as he has not found himself or has lost himself again. But *man* is not an abstract being, squatting outside the world. Man is *the human world*, the state, society. This state, this society, produce religion which is an *inverted world consciousness*, because they are an *inverted world*. Religion is the general theory of this world, its encyclopedic compendium, its logic in popular form, its spiritual *point d'honneur*, its enthusiasm, its moral sanction, its solemn complement, its general basis of consolation and justification. It is *the fantastic realization* of the human being inasmuch as the *human being* possesses no true reality. The struggle against religion is, therefore, indirectly a struggle against *that world* whose spiritual *aroma* is religion[3].

2.1. Note that although Marx's style appears to be rather journalistic, he does manage to compress a considerable philosophical load into his sentences. The journalistic pointedness is intended to make his readers sit up and take note. However, he does not thereby sacrifice depth, for his writing is at the same time characterized by a compactness that intends to make it clear to the reader that the author is a philosopher who has thought deeply on many questions and problems. These

---

[3] *Ibid.*, p. 43.

remarks on style may seem somewhat beside the point, but they form a rationale for our method of proceeding, namely, by a detailed exegesis of the text.

2.2.   The self-assured style of the opening sentences issues out of their being based on the work of Feuerbach, a post-Hegelian philosopher whose critique of religion, in *The Essence of Christianity*, was an attempt to refute Christianity. He explained that religion is just a *projection* of man himself motivated by the fact that certain needs in man's life remain unsatisfied. Although only man himself can satisfy his own needs, because he feels that he cannot satisfy them immediately, he projects himself into another world as an ideal being whose needs have been fully satisfied: this being man calls God. This, in a nutshell, is Feuerbach's analysis of religion. Feuerbach went on to say that as soon as religion is analysed and unmasked, there is no longer any need for such an ideal being. Man can once again become himself; instead of being attached to this ideal being called God, he can assume full reality for himself. Theology has, thus, become anthropology. He can confront his needs realistically, for he now knows that he is dependent upon his fellow man for his satisfaction. Instead of a sterile escape to religion and God, man in solidarity with his fellowman can now work at means by which to satisfy present and pressing needs. For our purpose, it is not necessary to dwell on Feuerbach any further, since the elements of Feuerbach's analysis relevant to Marx are brought out adequately by Marx himself in the passage we just quoted.

The point that Marx makes in the second paragraph is this: since the world of beautiful semblance, i.e., the upper world of heaven, and the human inclination toward that upper world have been unmasked (mainly by Feuerbach), and since the fantastic world of supernatural being has been denounced as escape fiction or as a subterfuge, now there is less chance that man can avoid or ignore the fact that he finds only a semblance of himself in this earthly reality. By this "semblance" Marx means error. And man can no longer avoid or escape from the fact of the existence of this error, from this semblance of himself, from this non-human being, because there is no place left to escape to, now that the fantastic upper world has been unmasked. Now man must face up to the existence of error, of this semblance, and of non-human being. In other words, philosophical critique, whose function it is to point out such error, can finally come into its own. Marx, thus, understands the word "error" in this context as being (more or less) human problems, needs and distresses, i.e., non-human being.

2.3.   The foregoing should become clearer by inquiring into how the key notions of "semblance" and "criticism" function in Marx's argument. But in order to make that inquiry more pointed, we must first answer the question: what does Marx mean when he says, in the first paragraph, that "the criticism of religion is the premise of all criticism"? (Another translation of the word used here and translated as "premise" might be "presupposition".) Marx seems to be giving a special import to religion in this statement. Otherwise, why would the criticism of religion be the premise of *all* criticism? But in what sense does it have special import? Marx's attempt to explain the phenomenon of religion by pointing to a given historical constellation suggests that it has a status similar to a historical phenomenon, except that it is more influential and more durable. However, this interpretation gives rise to new difficulties. For Marx's view involves another complicating factor: it includes a certain necessity within historical development itself. Thus, he explains the phenomenon of religion by pointing to that inner historical necessity. This is what he means when in the third paragraph quoted above he says:

> Religion is indeed man's self-consciousness and self-awareness so long as he has not found himself or has lost himself again. But *man* is not an abstract being, squatting outside the world. Man is *the human world*, the state, society. This state, this society, produce religion which is an *inverted world consciousness*, because they are an *inverted world*.

Thus, Marx does not want to just dismiss religion as a fiction, but wants to treat it as a historical phenomenon that can and must be explained. But how can Marx at the same time hope to offer a critique of religion, which involves pointing to a certain deviation from certain norms, if he views its development as being necessary? If, indeed, Marx is saying that although religion is an illusion, it was necessary in the development of history itself, then his critique is not really a critique, in the sense of a careful examination of religion, and certainly not in the sense of "the premise of all criticism". Rather, this interpretation seems to leave no alternative but to view religion *either* as something that needs to be abolished by forceful interference, *or* as something that can be expected to disappear "automatically" (in the course of historical events as such). In neither case does there seem to be any special need for theoretical criticism.

2.4. However, there is another possible way of interpreting Marx in which the difficulty we have raised could be avoided. In the long quotation given above we read: "The basis of irreligious criticism is this: *man makes religion*, religion does not make man". Marx, thus, seems to be saying that this is the ultimate, the final basis of irreligious criticism beyond which we cannot go. This is different from saying that religion is a necessary consequence of an inverted world. Marx says that even though certain factors of an "objective" historical constellation are involved, ultimately man himself is responsible for the fact, the illusion of religion. But if this is the ultimate fact of irreligious criticism, then, although Marx may want to call it a criticism, it really only amounts to a rejection of religion. The basic proposition that man makes religion seems to be on the same footing as the one that he wants to refute, namely, that religion makes man; for neither one is rooted in an appeal to the inner necessity of history. Since he does no more than posit this ultimate basis without accounting for it, Marx is doing nothing more than confronting one religious stance with another – his own.

2.5. But Marx goes on to make another point in the third paragraph of our quotation: "But *man* is not an abstract being, squatting outside the world". This statement is clearly a polemic against German Idealism. German Idealism conceives of man as a being that ultimately culminates in a spiritual idea. In Hegel, the state was the societal expression of this spiritual idea. This Marx wants to reject. Although his criticism may be correct, what does Marx gain when, in the next sentence, he replaces this idealization of man by *"the human world, the state, society"*? Although this statement may look concrete, actually it, too, is an abstraction. To present such an abstraction as concrete, even as pre-eminently so, results in nothing but mystification. In fact, it is a mystification that persists to the present day. It is a consequence of 19th century positivism *à la* Comte. This positivism posited over against idealistic sophistication and formalistic moralism the idea of society. Society with a capital "S" remained an ill-defined, vague, leveling idea. Therefore, it was hardly useful as a scientific concept. It is this mystification (still current) that reappears in Marx.

Besides this mystifying touch, Marx is here positing his real problems as being out in the *world* of history and society. He does this with the intention of being able to appeal to *man himself* at the moment that he offers his own positive ideas: at this moment, he has to be able to appeal to man as an active responsible being, rather than a being swept inexorably along by history (or escaping into the fantastic reality of heaven).

2.6. A quotation often used as a slogan by Marxists and often denounced by Christians is found at the end of the following passage taken from Marx's essay:

> *Religious* suffering is at the same time an *expression* of real suffering and a *protest* against real suffering. Religion is the sigh of the oppressed creature, the sentiment of a heartless world, and the soul of soulless conditions. It is the *opium* of the people[4].

It is important that we examine the context of this much-quoted statement; otherwise, it appears more simple than it really is. By the metaphor "opium" Marx means that religion both hides and reveals the real suffering and needs of the people. He calls it "an *expression* of

[4] *Ibid.*, pp. 43, 44.

35

real suffering and a *protest* against real suffering". But, at the same time, it is an illusion, a kind of drug which, although revealing these needs and sufferings, is also a concealment of and an escape from them. Marx himself does not use it as a superficial slogan: he wants to take religion seriously because it is an expression of real needs and suffering, but, at the same time, a mistaken and unsuccessful expression, one that fails.

The following quotation further elucidates this dual attitude of Marx toward religion:

> The abolition of religion as the *illusory* happiness of men, is a demand for their *real* happiness. The call to abandon their illusions about their condition is a *call to abandon a condition which requires illusions*. The criticism of religion is, therefore, *the embryonic criticism of this vale of tears* of which religion is the *halo*[5].

Here Marx posits Feuerbach's critique of religion as the germ, the embryo of a full-blown critique of society. It is also clear from this passage that criticism and practical intervention become closely related; indeed, they merge. Marx abandons the term criticism (in the sense of unmasking it as a semblance and illusion) and speaks here of the abolition of religion. However, this concept of abolition is also drawn from German Idealism: it is a translation of that term, so important in German Idealism – *aufheben*.

2.7.   At this point, we should perhaps explain what is meant by the term "aufheben" and how it functions in the dialectical logic of idealism. In traditional logic "A is not" is the negation of "A is". But according to Hegel, we cannot leave it at this simple opposition: when we combine the two statements "A is A" and "A is not non-A", we bring out a certain sameness or "identity" of "A" which "transcends" the simple opposition of "being" and "non-being". This *Aufhebung* of the opposition (indicated by the twofold use of "not") can be expressed in the statement "A becomes". But the "Aufhebung" is not just a simple negation of this opposition (or negation) between "A is" and "A is not"; it is also a synthesis. Thus, it is a synthesizing negation; for, while abolishing the opposition it also preserves it, since "A becomes" implies simultaneously that "A is" and that "A is not".

Marx, however, tries to detach the concept of "Aufhebung" from its Hegelian context. With Hegel it appears in a theoretical context; in a way, he tries to prove this dialectical logic logically. Marx tries to detach the concept of abolition from that theoretical context; for him, it is the breakthrough of a tenacious illusion, not just a synthesizing negation in the above logical sense. (Yet he still wants to suggest the same "logical" cogency that Hegel, following a long tradition in this

[5] *Ibid.*, p. 44.

36

respect, wanted to maintain). Accordingly, this abolition is also a practical demand for the replacement of illusion by reality.

2.8. Behind this demand there resides in Marx the postulate of man's striving for happiness. To explain this, we have to refer back to Marx's view of religion. Religion for all its illusoriness is a human product, and as such it has a certain reality. It is an utterance, a manifestation of something from which man cannot escape. However, it is an erroneous expression, it fails, so it has to be abolished. But, since religion is a manifestation of something from which man cannot escape, it immediately needs a substitute. This "something" is Marx's postulate of man's striving for happiness: man as such has to strive for happiness.

Religion failed at the attempt to fulfill the requirement of this postulate, so it has to be replaced. At the beginning of this essay, philosophy appeared as destructive criticism; it had to break through the illusion of religion. But now philosophy appears as a positive demand based on the postulate of happiness. Furthermore, this positive demand amounts to a call *"to abandon a condition which requires illusions"*. Thus, it is not so much a call to introspective reflection, for example, on the import and impact of man's moral conscience (à la Kant). Nor is it a call to come to an awareness of the significance of oneself as a human subject that is wholly activity (à la Fichte). It is important to note Marx's difference from these calls or postulates; for, although he is an heir to this tradition of German Idealism, he introduces a major change. Thus, Marx calls upon man to intervene practically in a condition of which he has become the victim, a condition which could only lead him into illusions, semblances and fictions. The only way out for Marx is not that of self-reflection or of the intensification of the sense of responsibility, but the way of efficacious action.

2.9. The following passage expresses Marx's call in brilliant metaphorical language:

> Criticism has plucked the imaginary flowers from the chain, not in order that man shall bear the chain without caprice or consolation but so that he shall cast of the chains and pluck the living flower. The criticism of religion disillusions man so that he will think, act and fashion his reality as a man who has lost his illusions and regained his reason; so that he will revolve about himself as his own true sun. Religion is only the illusory sun about which man revolves so long as he does not revolve about himself[6].

Note that he speaks of living flowers and the sun; we could say he is tuned in to spring: he is not yet using the grim language of his later development, a language which would rather have to be characterized as being tuned in to autumn. However, even here it appears that this

[6] *Ibid.*, p. 44.

bright spring can only be found after losing one's illusions. The emphasis falls on the latter part of the passage: "The criticism of religion disillusions man so that he will think, act and fashion his reality as a man who has lost his illusions and regained his reason; so that he will revolve about himself as his own true sun". We seldom find such a clear statement of the essence of humanism. Although it is a very clear and striking formulation, it is not a particularly critical one; that is, Marx neither tries to prove or account for its truth. To put it more pointedly, Marx has in no way explained why the content of his stated ideal of man revolving about himself "as his own true sun" is superior to what he takes to be the illusion of religion. Thus, it is just another dogmatic statement, not a critical one. We may even call it a confession. (This is all we can say while still staying within the limits of philosophical argument. But if we go beyond these limits, then as a believer and confessor one has to oppose one's own confession to that of Marx. Then this statement amounts to the most fundamental and tragic illusion of man, especially of modern and contemporary man – an illusion in which we are all inclined to believe, even as Christians. This is, perhaps, the hardest struggle of the Christian in Western society.)

2.10.   But we must move on in our attempt to answer the question whether Marx ever rises, as he wishes to, above a simple dismissal of religion. In this connection, we quote a passage that is vital to the course of Marx's argument; it presents us with his notion of truth:

> It is the *task of history*, therefore, once the *other-world of truth* has vanished, to establish the *truth of this world*. The immediate *task of philosophy*, which is in the service of history, is to unmask human self-alienation in its *secular form* now that it has been unmasked in its *sacred form*. Thus the criticism of heaven is transformed into the criticism of earth, the *criticism of religion* into the *criticism of law*, and the *criticism of theology* into the *criticism of politics*[7].

The phrases, "*other-world of truth*" and "*truth of this world*" are evidence of Marx's continuing concern for truth. Truth is characterized by its opposition to the "*other-world of truth*", which is the semblance, the fantastic, fictitious world of heaven. But we also detect what is a general feature of dialectical thought as such: besides being opposed to each other, truth and what seems to be truth (the semblance) are also related to each other. The self-imposed task of dialectical thought is, by bringing out this oppositional relationship as strongly and sharply as possible, to finally arrive at a stronger affirmation of the ultimate and total truth. This affirmation claims to be so powerful that even semblance, despite its negativity and untruth, can be accounted for and, in a sense, assimilated so as to become part of this total truth. In this regard, a question presses itself upon us: could this not be interpreted

---

[7] *Ibid.*, p. 44.

relativistically? If untruth becomes part of truth as a whole, what criterion is left by which to judge whether something is true or untrue? Nevertheless, this is what Marx tries to do with religion. Despite its illusoriness, its negativity and untruth, Marx attempts to see it as part of the truth. This concern for truth on the part of Marx stands out even more plainly when we compare him in this respect to another German philosopher who succeeded him, Friedrich Nietzsche.

2.11.   Although it may seem a digression to introduce Nietzsche at this point, Marx and Nietzsche are so often treated in combination, especially with regard to their criticism of the other-world of religion, that a comparison can only be instructive. Although they have this critique of religion in common, they differ in their concern for truth. Take, for example, two of Nietzsche's well-known aphorisms: "Let's make an experiment with truth", and, "Truth is a kind of error which certain living beings need for living". Nietzsche has here given up the concern for truth as an ultimate concern. However, if we recall the observation we made with regard to the relativistic possibility inherent in Marx's dialectical way of speaking about truth, we will detect a certain continuity. If, indeed, untruth is finally a part of truth, then we are left open to the complete relativism of Nietzsche: truth as an experiment, and truth as a kind of error. When Marx says, "It is the *task of history* . . . to establish the truth of this world", he displays a concern that Nietzsche has abandoned; for Nietzsche must even refuse the attempt to establish truth in a possible future, that is, from a horizontal eschatological perspective, because, unlike Marx, he denies that such a perspective is possible. According to him, "Reality is an eternal recurrence of the same". Thus, a projection of any kind makes no sense at all. Perhaps this is the final consequence of the phrase we quoted from Marx regarding man revolving about himself as his own sun. However, Marx does not go this far; he is still concerned with truth as a real value.

2.12.   Returning once again to the passage we quoted above, we read: "It is the *task of history*, therefore, once the other-world of truth has vanished, to establish the *truth of this world*". What is the notion of history that is operative in this sentence? History for Marx is a process of continual change, a succession of different phases that alternate and sometimes temporarily clash. To both Hegel and Marx transition is a crucial notion of history. It is a movement from the "not yet" to the "no longer"; thus, it is seen as both a separation and a connection simultaneously. This peculiar character must be grasped by means of dialectic, the method of opposition and abolition of opposition. "A becomes" means that "A" is in a process of transition; we might say it is born out of an opposition, namely, the opposition between "A is" and "A is not". Although this dialectical method was already the property of the German Idealists, for them, as for Hegel, from the beginning there was no doubt that history as a process of change, of continual transition, was a history of the thinking, reflecting mind. Thus, to them it was possible to comprehend the whole process philosophically. Of course, philosophical methodology had to be adjusted to comprehend the movement of history; indeed, a new method, a truly dialectical method had to be created. But, ultimately, a philosophical comprehension of history was not problematical because history itself was the history of the thinking mind. But now Marx comes along and says that it is the task of history itself to establish truth; in the final analysis, history posits its own task. Marx does not introduce philosophy until the second sentence of the quoted passage: he begins, "The immediate *task of philosophy*", and immediately adds, "which is in the service of history". This is consistent with the first statement of the passage. Using an analogy, we could say that history appears as the chief instructor and philosophy as its servant.

2.13. From the perspective of the development of Marx's thought, we can note a slight difference between this and his original position. The latter we discussed in connection with the annotations to his dissertation (1841). At that time, he stated that the theoretical mind passes into will as praxis; that philosophy becomes worldly by becoming involved in the historical process; but philosophy still remains a certain development of the theoretical mind. Thus, his starting point then was still the theoretical mind. Whereas now, returning to the quote at hand (1843), history as such has first place; nevertheless, this statement also immediately poses a task for philosophy. The critique of religion has determined that henceforth the truth of this world is at stake, and since philosophy, in the service of history, first establishes this truth, now, as Marx says in the quoted passage, the critique of law and of politics becomes its major task. Thus we see that the argument of this essay leads to a critique of Hegel's *Philosophy of Right*, which is a philosophical task. Accordingly, this change does not mean that Marx has made a real break with his previous view of the role of philosophy, for a certain continuity is also preserved. But a real shift in emphasis has clearly taken place, so that now history is primary, philosophy being in its service.

3. *Marx's Encounter with the German Situation*

However, in the passage succeeding the quotation we have been dealing with, it becomes clear that a certain limitation of philosophy's task (to aid history in the establishing of truth) does take place:

The following exposition – which is a contribution to this undertaking – does

40

not deal directly with the original but with a copy, the German *philosophy* of the state and of right, for the simple reason that it deals with Germany[8].

In the preceding paragraph, we read that "the criticism of heaven is transformed into the criticism of earth, the *criticism of religion* into the *criticism of law*, and the *criticism of theology* into the *criticism of politics*". So the "original" referred to here is law and politics as they are in themselves, while the "copy" is the German *philosophy* of the state and of right. Thus, the task of philosophy is limited by a certain uniquely German situation. Here we have come to the second main point that we said had to be dealt with in order to come to an adequate understanding of Marx's argument. We have thus far been dealing with the first point, the critique of religion; now Marx's special concern with Germany must be introduced.

3.1.   In response to the quoted passage, we might ask Marx, why is it not possible to go right on into a critique of the original? Marx's phrasing suggests that this might be possible, e.g., in the case of England and France, but not in the case of Germany. Instead, here one has to start with the copy, with philosophy, rather than with the original. This is so because of the peculiar level of historical development attained by Germany. We may recall that Marx sees history as a sort of chief instructor; consequently, it is necessary to keep pace with the level of historical development. But how is the necessity of dealing with a copy a consequence of the obligation to keep up with history? In order to answer this, we have to refer to a passage further on in the same essay, where Marx states:

> We are the *philosophical* contemporaries of the present day without being its *historical* contemporaries. German philosophy is the *ideal prolongation* of German history[9].

And also:

> The German *philosophy of right and of the state* is the only German history which is *al pari* with the *official* modern times[10].

And finally in addressing himself to a certain party in Germany:

> You demand as a point of departure real germs of life, but you forget that the real germ of life of the German nation has so far sprouted only in its *cranium*[11].

He is saying that a direct criticism of the political and social *status quo* in Germany would amount to an anachronism. This becomes obvious in the following passage:

[8] *Ibid.*, p. 44.
[9] *Ibid.*, p. 49.
[10] *Ibid.*, p. 50.
[11] *Loc. cit.*

If one were to start with the *status quo* itself [that is to say the original: law and politics] in Germany, even in the most appropriate way, i.e. negatively [critically], the result would still be an *anachronism*. Even the negation of our political present is already a dusty fact in the historical lumber room of modern nations[12].

3.2.   Thus, Marx's reason for concentration on the German philosophy of the state and of right, rather than the state and right themselves, is that this is the only point at which Germany has reached a level comparable to other nations. What does this reasoning imply? If it is true that Germany is modern only in its philosophy, and if philosophy is only a copy of an original, i.e., of the socio-political situation itself, then in this case, strange as it may seem, the copy is ahead of the original. In other words, the copy sets the tone for historical development. Furthermore, his argument implies a distinction between German history and other national histories, and finally, a distinction between different levels of development within "History" (as a whole). These levels exist in a value relationship to each other; accordingly, he can speak of an "anachronism" and say that "even the negation of our political present is already a dusty fact in the historical lumber room of modern nations".

3.3.   The need for distinguishing national histories and, more importantly, different historical levels, seems to point to the fact that the concept of history cannot fulfill the role of most universal and comprehensive concept; in other words, it reveals the insufficiency of the conception of history as chief instructor. History is an empty concept unless special distinctions are introduced, like those of national histories and, especially, evaluative concepts. Without these (more than merely historical) standards, history in becoming comprehensive also becomes empty of meaning.

Marx's battle cry to join in a war against the state of affairs in Germany also reveals the inadequacy of history as an ultimate concept. Marx does not mean this figuratively; he means a literal, violent battle, as becomes clear when he says:

> But *war* upon the state of affairs in Germany! By all means! This state of affairs is *beneath the level of history, beneath all criticism*; nevertheless it remains an object of criticism just as the criminal who is beneath humanity remains an object of the *executioner*. In its struggle against this state of affairs criticism is not a passion of the head, but the head of passion. It is not a lancet but a weapon. Its object is an *enemy* which it aims not to refute but to *destroy*. For the spirit of this state of affairs has already been refuted. It is not, in itself, an object worthy of our thought; it is an *existence* as contemptible as it is despised. Criticism itself has no need of any further elucidation of this object, for it has already understood it. Criticism is no longer an end in itself, but simply a means: *indignation* is its essential mode of feeling, and *denunciation* its principal task[13].

[12] *Ibid.*, pp. 44-45.
[13] *Ibid.*, p. 46.

So, although it is beneath the level of history, this German state of affairs is yet real enough to deserve passionate opposition. With merely the concept of history as a standard, Marx would not be able to pronounce judgement on the contemporary German situation.

3.4. The concept of passion (*Leidenschaft*) as it functions in this passage induces a new meaning into the term "criticism" that Marx also uses here: criticism comes to mean a direct, vehement and passionate reaction. The term "criticism" would not be suitable here except in this new sense, because the state of affairs in Germany is beneath the level of criticism. Marx goes on to say that, "nevertheless it remains an object of criticism just as the criminal who is beneath humanity remains an object of the *executioner*". The kind of criticism that is appropriate "is not a passion of the head, but the head of passion". Thus, in this new sense criticism becomes an existential criticism, a direct, vehement and passionate reaction, because human existence is affected immediately and profoundly by the object of this criticism. The object is a state of affairs that is intolerable and that, therefore, incites man to direct and total action.

Our understanding of Marx's notion of passion can benefit from comparison with the notion of passion held by one of his contemporaries: that unique and remarkable philosopher Sören Kierkegaard. Kierkegaard, too, was a great critic of Hegelianism and of bourgeois society; however, he directed his criticism not so much at its economic and political aspects as at its manifestation in the church. Nevertheless, an interesting similarity does exist with regard to their notion of passion. It is a key notion also for Kierkegaard; for, according to him, a person is only authentically and completely himself in passion. In passion a person is affected by something other; he is affected so profoundly that immediately a full existential reaction is provoked in him, which involves action. Thus, in passion, passivity and activity join each other. However, although Kierkegaard and Marx do have this notion of passion in common, a difference does exist. For, whereas Kierkegaard's passion is ultimately motivated by the fact that man is or should be in the service of God, we have found Marx's passion to be motivated by the fact that man is or should be in the service of *history*. We have also found that his concept of history as the chief instructor proved to be inadequate and ambiguous.

Interestingly enough, a similar ambiguity occurs in Kierkegaard, for he did not only say that he was in the service of God, he also added that he was in the *secret* service of God. He called himself a spy of God. This ambiguity is inevitable according to Kierkegaard, because there is something profoundly paradoxical in his chief "instructor" (God) himself. For God has chosen to reveal himself by concealment. In fact, He chose not only the way of concealment, but also that of absurdity, namely, the way of Jesus Christ. Threre is eternal truth in God's revelation, but it is concentrated in the historical person of Jesus Christ. But how is this concentration of eternal truth in a merely historical person possible? Is this not an absurdity? But these comments are sufficient to give us some idea of the similarities and differences between the notions of passion of Marx and Kierkegaard.

3.5. Returning to our comments on the passage quoted above, we read: "Criticism is no longer an end in itself, but simply a means". That is to say, the state of affairs in Germany can no longer be ignored, but must be criticized, and this criticism is the utterance of a sacred indignation. Thus, it is no longer an end in itself, but a means to the radical destruction of this state of affairs. It cannot be a cool, detached criticism, but passes over into a kind of reign of terror:

> The criticism which deals with this subject-matter [that state of affairs] is criticism in a hand-to-hand fight; and in such a fight it is of no interest to know whether the adversary is of the same rank, is noble or *interesting* – all that matters is to *strike* him[14].

Marx continues on the same page, describing the function of criticism in terms of keeping the German populace in a state of constant terror:

> It is a question of denying the Germans an instant of illusion or resignation. The burden must be made still more irksome by awakening a consciousness of it, and shame must be made more shameful still by rendering it public. Every sphere of German society must be depicted as the *partie honteuse* of German society; and these petrified social conditions must be made to dance by singing their own melody to them. The nation must be taught to be *terrified* of itself, in order to give it *courage*. In this way an imperious need of the German nation will be satisfied, and the needs of nations are themselves the final cause of their satisfaction[15].

Here criticism has come to mean simply an activity that aims at complete practical destruction.

3.6. But this criticism, which is really no longer a criticism but a hand-to-hand combat against the immediate German situation, is not limited in its scope to just that situation; it has a universal purpose as well. As Marx puts it:

> Even for the modern nations this struggle against the limited character of the German *status quo* does not lack interest; for the German *status quo* is the open *consummation of the ancien régime*, and the *ancien régime* is the *hidden defect of the modern state*. The struggle against the political present of the Germans is a struggle against the past of the modern nations, who are still continually importuned by the reminiscences of this past. It is instructive for the modern nations to see the *ancien régime*, which has played a *tragic* part in their history, play a *comic* part as a German ghost. The *ancien régime* had

---

[14] *Ibid.*, p. 47.
[15] *Loc. cit.*

a *tragic* history, so long as it was the established power in the world while liberty was a personal fancy; in short, so long as it believed and had to believe in its own validity. So long as the *ancien régime*, as an existing world order, struggled against a new world which was just coming into existence, there was on its side a historical error but no personal error. Its decline was, therefore, tragic.

The present German régime, on the other hand, which is an anachronism, a flagrant contradiction of universally accepted axioms – the nullity of the *ancien régime* revealed to the whole world – only imagines that it believes in itself and asks the world to share its illusion[16].

Thus, Marx discovers the universal purpose of his criticism in the fact that, "the German *status quo* is the *open consummation of the ancien régime*, and the *ancien régime* is the *hidden defect of the modern state*". However, this argument can be sustained only if Marx presupposes a still more complex concept of history than he has shown thus far. Marx further explains himself by saying that modern nations "are still continually importuned by the reminiscences of this past". In other words, the past of modern nations is still present; in fact, it is present as a hidden defect of the modern state. This implies that Marx's concept of the "reached" level of historical development as the official level of history has become more complicated than at first appeared; the past is still operative in this level. Only on the basis of this presence of the past is Marx able to claim a universal purpose for his criticism of the particular German situation. The particular German situation or *status quo* derives its universality mainly from its negativity; for Marx's criticism shows it to be the epitome of the "nullity of the *ancien régime*". Germany, thus, serves as an instructive reminder and warning to all other nations regarding the nullity of the *ancien régime*. But, of course, this nullity cannot then be absolute. It could not serve as a reminder, as a present defect in the modern state, if it did not possess a reality of some sort. In fact, one would think it would have to possess a striking sort of reality.

3.7. However, although Marx's criticism derives its universality mainly from negativity, the nullity of the *ancien régime*, it also has a positive aspect. Thus, Marx argues that this hand-to-hand combat against a particular situation, although it seems so limited in its scope, actually possesses a two-fold universality: in the previously stated negative sense, but also in a positive sense. Marx sketches this positive aspect as follows:

If it believed in its own *nature* would it attempt to hide it beneath the *semblance* of an alien nature and look for its salvation in hypocrisy and sophistry? The modern *ancien régime* is the comedian of a world order whose *real heros* are dead. History is thorough, and it goes through many stages when it conducts an ancient formation to its grave. The last stage of a world-

[16] *Ibid.*, pp. 47-48.

historical formation is comedy. The Greek gods, already once mortally wounded in Aeschylus' tragedy *Prometheus Bound*, had to endure a second death, a comic death, in Lucian's dialogues. Why should history proceed in this way? So that mankind shall separate itself *gladly* from its past. We claim this *joyful* historical destiny for the political powers of Germany[17].

Thus, Marx divides history into two main stages: a tragic stage followed by a comic stage. While the past tragic stage had real tragic heroes – the heroes of the *ancien régime* –, the comic stage has no heroes. This is the situation in which Germany finds itself. Although this comic stage in which Germany occurs has no heroes, it nevertheless has a real function, not only to Germany, but also to mankind as a whole. Despite its negativity, the German situation is amusing; and in beholding it, mankind is enabled to gladly separate itself from its past which it sees there. Clever as this construct may be, it does seem to have a decadent flavor. For the gaity that Marx assumes here clashes sharply with the note of strident indignation he sounded just before; consequently, his gaity sounds phony.

Marx's conception of the comic again begs for comparison with Kierkegaard. Kierkegaard, too, represented his time and the Hegelian philosophy of his time in very negative terms. Like Marx, he also tried to give this negative situation a positive ring by pointing out the comic in it. Sometimes his sense of the comic seems to be a desperate attempt to say something positive about a situation that he actually experienced as intolerable and as demanding a radically negative critique. Hegel had located such negativity within a systematic framework of dialectical thought. This was impossible for Kierkegaard: he experienced the negative reality, the intolerableness of the situation too existentially to dispense with it so easily. Yet, he tried to temper his sense for the negativity of the situation by evoking the comic. Kierkegaard's notion of the comic is more developed than that of Marx, for he distinguishes the comical, the ironical and the humorous. The latter, the sense of humor, contains a genuine religious strain according to Kierkegaard. There are more differences involved between Marx's and Kierkegaard's notions of the comic, but this must suffice to give us some idea of how the notion functioned in their respective critiques.

3.8.   So far, we have been concerned with following Marx's argument as he demonstrates the universal purpose of his passionate criticism. But, although Marx wanted to point out that even this kind of criticism of Germany was relevant to the situation of the other nations, his critical attention is aimed at "the arrears" of Germany in particular.

17 *Ibid.*, p. 48.

But as soon as criticism concerns itself with modern social and political reality, and thus arrives at genuine human problems, it must either go outside the German *status quo* or approach its object indirectly [via philosophy][18].

And also,

While in France and England the problem is put in the form: *political economy* or the *rule of society over wealth*; in Germany it is put in the form: *national economy* or the *rule of private property over nationality*[19].

Here he points out that in comparison to Germany, France and England are much more progressive. Marx adds that,

If the *whole* of German development were at the level of German *political* development, a German could have no greater part in contemporary problems than can a *Russian*[20].

An ironical sentence, indeed, in the light of historical developments since then! But Marx never anticipated the impact his ideas were to have, especially on Russia. However, there is one aspect of German culture that elevates it to an equal level with the other countries: its philosophy. As Marx puts it:

Just as the nations of the ancient world lived their pre-history in the imagination, in mythology, so we Germans have lived our post-history in thought, in *philosophy*[21].

Here Marx is again picking up the theme he initiated earlier with his statement: "The following exposition ... does not deal directly with the original [i.e., with the state and society as such] but with a copy, [namely] the German philosophy of the state and of right, for the simple reason that it deals with Germany".[22] And, he comes to a clear statement of why it is necessary to deal first with philosophy, given the German situation:

We are the *philosophical* contemporaries of the present day without being its *historical* contemporaries. German philosophy is the *ideal prolongation* of German history[23].

Because in its philosophy German is on a par with the other nations, Marx's critical discussion of German philosophy is not just a *particular* discussion limited to Germany; but it indirectly has a kind of *exemplary* value for the criticism of the modern historical situation as a whole and for the human problems involved in that situation. Thus, the indirect approach that Marx points to in introducing the above quoted state-

---

[18] *Ibid.*, p. 48.
[19] *Ibid.*, p. 49.
[20] *Loc. cit.*
[21] *Loc. cit.*
[22] *Ibid.*, p. 44.
[23] *Ibid.*, p. 49.

ments with the words, "But as as soon as criticism concerns itself with modern social and political reality ..., it must either go outside the German *status quo* or approach its object indirectly",[24] consists of a general critique by way of German philosophy.

3.9. However, the general rule formulated by Marx was that philosophy has to be considered as a copy of the original, i.e., of the historical situation. Then this exemplary function of German philosophy can only be sustained at the expense of accepting a deviation from this general rule. For in the German situation there is no original at all, only a copy; but if there is no original, then one cannot really speak of a copy either. Marx sums it up thus:

> That which constitutes, for the advanced nations, a *practical* break with modern political conditions, is in Germany where these conditions do not yet exist, virtually a *critical* break with their philosophical reflection[25].

This sentence clearly states that the historical conditions in Germany do not yet exist, so it is strange that German philosophy could be called a copy of the original. Nevertheless, the main point that Marx wants to make here is that historically speaking a critical break with German philosophy has the same value in Germany as a practical break had in the other countries. In other words, a criticism of philosophy in Germany plays the same practical historical role as did the political conditions in other countries.

In the preceding argument Marx has prepared the ground in order to give himself free rein for a critique of German philosophy which would simultaneously be able to lay claim to practical relevance and importance for other nations as well. But as long as Marx maintains that philosophy as such in Germany be called a copy of an original, and that his critical approach be indirect, then this free rein is no longer really free. Marx himself will feel the difficulties involved in this attempt to "kill two birds with one stone".

3.10. Marx carries his argument a step further into even greater complexity:

> The German *philosophy of right and of the state* is the only German history which is *al pari* with the *official* modern times. The German nation is obliged, therefore, to connect its dream history [i.e., German philosophy] with its present conditions, and to subject to criticism not only these existing conditions but also their abstract continuation [philosophy]. Its future cannot be restricted either to the direct negation of its real juridical and political circumstances, or to the direct realization of its ideal juridical and political circumstances [right and state]. The direct negation of its real circumstances already exists in its ideal circumstances [philosophy of right and state], while it has almost outlived the realization of its ideal circumstances in the contempla-

[24] *Ibid.*, p .48.
[25] *Ibid.*, p. 50.

This statement reminds us of the annotations to his dissertation, where he points out that philosophy had to become practical energy: "philosophy becoming worldly and the world becoming philosophical". Marx is saying the same thing here: "the direct negation of its real circumstances already *exists* in its ideal circumstances",[27] that is to say, the philosophy of right and of the state has to be considered as a direct negation of the German situation. This parallels the observation in the annotations that Hegelian philosophy has to be considered as practical energy which makes contact with reality in a negative critical sense. Note the added emphasis on the word "exists" in the quoted passage: the German philosophy of the state and of right is *part* of the whole of contemporary German historical reality; it is this alone that makes German history comparable with and equal to the historical level of other nations. Thus, German philosophy of right and of the state exists in the present as part of the situation as a whole; but at the same time it is also a negation of that historical situation. Consequently, we cannot stay in the present, but are forced to inquire into the future. In Marx's words, this German philosophy of right and of the state can be considered as the realization of Germany's ideal circumstances, which are also the direct negation of the present situation. But this existing negation is in need of a new negation.

Summing up, we have: first, a direct negation in the German philosophy of right and of the state which belongs to German reality as a whole and puts it on a par with other nations; secondly, the need for a new negation in the future in order to make progress possible. Germany has almost outlived this realization of its ideal circumstances in the contemplation of neighboring nations. Because other nations progress by way of a practical break with their modern political conditions and because Germany is on a par with these nations only in that existing direct negation, i.e., in its philosophy, Germany must necessarily break with its philosophy just to keep pace with the progress of the other nations. Herein lies the need for a negation of the existing negation. Marx's argument is concluded in the statement: "It is with good reason, therefore, that the practical political party in Germany demands the negation of philosophy". In other words, Marx agrees with the demands of the practical political party for the negation of philosophy. The argument we have been tracing explains the reasons for his agreement.

3.11. However, Marx also indicates a point of disagreement with the demands of this political party:

[26] *Ibid.*, p. 50.
[27] *Ibid.*, p. 50 [italics added].

Its error does not consist in formulating this demand, but in limiting itself to a demand which it does not, and cannot, make effective. It supposes that it can achieve this negation by turning its back on philosophy, looking elsewhere, and murmuring a few trite and ill-humoured phrases. Because of its narrow outlook it does not take account of philosophy as part of *German* reality, and even regards philosophy as beneath the level of German practical life and its theories. You demand as a point of departure real germs of life [a vivid revolutionary movement], but you forget that the real germ of life of the German nation has so far sprouted only in its *cranium*. In short, *you cannot abolish philosophy without realizing it*[28].

The error of the party can be interpreted in two ways, the first of which is the more abstract. In this interpretation, starting from the agreed point of view that philosophy is in need of a new negation, Marx adds a qualification: this political party does not sufficiently realize that this new negation has to remain a negation of a negation. This party, says Marx, thought to achieve this negation by turning its back on philosophy. In the terms of Hegelian dialectics which he utilizes here, Marx points out that this is impossible because the negation of the negation keeps referring to the negation which it negates. In a way, it continues it by way of negating it. The *negation* has to negate the former negation because the first negated negation is only a negation of a primary *positive* (pro)position. Given the primary proposition "A is", then "A is not" is the first negation. Although this phrases it in terms of a logical proposition, it is intended to refer also to real positions and historical situations. In the latter instance, "A is" refers to a certain historical establishment, and "A is not" refers to the negation of that establishment. But in Hegelian dialectics, this first negation is *only* a point and nothing more than a negation of the original positive proposition; as such, it does not say or *produce* anything of its own. What it says or produces can only be brought out by pointing back to the original proposition. In other words, it leads a parasitic kind of existence. Thus, in order to make it say or produce something of its own, the negation has to be *continued* in a negation *of the* negation; only then are we able to account for real change and progress in historical society. With the first negation alone ("A is not"), real historical *change* or *progress* cannot be accounted for. The entire content of the first negation can only be brought out by pointing back to the original position or proposition, in other words, by also conserving the established situation. Although this is a rather abstract and puzzling explanation involving many logical problems, it does expose the reasoning underlying Marx's argument.

However, there is another easier and less abstract way of interpreting the error committed by the aforementioned political party in its slogan demanding the negation of philosophy. Even if the slogan is

[28] *Ibid.*, p. 50.

true, it ignores the significance and function of the to-be-negated German philosophy as a practical historical power. Philosophy has to be criticized and even negated, but it cannot be simply left out.

3.12. In summary, it has become clear that Marx, in agreement with this political party, demands a negation of philosophy as philosophy. Previously, in the annotations to his dissertation, he already spoke of a certain inner defect of philosophy and a crisis in philosophy, but here, a few years later, his formulations are becoming more radical and demanding. He even speaks of the abolition of philosophy. However, he goes on to maintain that, "you cannot abolish philosophy without realizing it".

This abolition of philosophy requires acknowledgment of its powerful reality, at least in the German situation. We previously heard Marx say that theoretical mind or Hegelian philosophy had to pass into practical energy. In that context, we pointed out that although Marx wishes to indicate a certain defect in philosophy, he took his point of departure in that very philosophy, maintaining that it was philosophy as such that had to make a change. But even now, in his more radical idea of the abolition or negation of philosophy, Marx still clings to the conviction that it is philosophy as philosophy that demands realization and acknowledgment.

3.13. But now examine the reverse side of the coin. Following the course of Marx's argument, we read:

> The same error was committed, but in the opposite direction, by the *theoretical* party which originated in philosophy.
>
> In the present struggle, this party saw *only* the *critical struggle of philosophy against the German world*. It did not consider that *previous philosophy* itself belongs to this world and is its complement, even if only an ideal complement. Critical as regards its counterpart, it was not self-critical. It took as its point of departure the *presuppositions* of philosophy; and either accepted the conclusions which philosophy had reached or else presented as direct philosophical demands and conclusions, demands and conclusions drawn from elsewhere. But these latter – assuming their legitimacy – can only be achieved by the *negation of previous philosophy*, that is, philosophy as philosophy. We shall provide later a more comprehensive account of this party. Its principal defect may be summarized as follows: *it believed that it could realize philosophy without abolishing it*[29].

In addressing himself to the theoretical party, Marx means the followers of German Idealistic philosophy, seen as the continuation of Kantian criticism. They were right in emphasizing the *critical* strain and intention of this philosophy, says Marx, since it was only along this road that Germany reached the official level of modern history. One important point of Marx's criticism of that theoretical party is that, granted that this philosophy was capable of self-criticism, yet it was

[29] *Ibid.*, pp. 50-51.

still not self-critical enough. If that German Idealistic philosophy had been radical in its self-criticism, then it should have made the discovery which Marx made, namely, that it is impossible to "realize philosophy without abolishing it". According to Marx, German philosophy fell short of its own standards and its own possibilities.

3.14.   This lack of self-criticism amounts to the fact that "it took as its point of departure the *presuppositions* of philosophy". With this Marx seems to have in mind the traditional and permanent presuppositions of the Cartesian *cogito – sum*, I think – I am, which remains also the point of departure for the German Idealists; in the words of Hegel, there is an identity of thought and being. We say that Marx *"seems"* to have in mind such presuppositions, because the denotation of the term is not very clear. More important, even such presuppositions as the Cartesian *cogito – sum* demand a critical investigation. The real meaning of the *cogito – sum*, for example, can only be discovered by asking the question, what in the *existing* situation brought Descartes and his followers to their particular presupposition? A much quoted statement of Marx implies the same thing: he says that it is not consciousness which determines being but being which determines consciousness; or, it is not *cogito* that determines *sum*, but *sum* that determines *cogito*. This statement may seem like a simple reversal of, for example, the position of Descartes and the German Idealists, but Marx wants to argue that this statement expresses a more profound self-criticism of philosophy, especially of its presuppositions. At the same time, we must note that Marx's inquiry into the "existing situation" immediately orients him to the historical world. This is the particular presupposition of Marx himself and his basis for judging other philosophers. We can rephrase Marx's question thus: what in the historical world brought, e.g., Descartes, to such presuppositions? Thus, Marx is asking what kind of ontology is implied in the seemingly epistemological (*cogito*) approach of Descartes. Marx reproaches the theoretical party for neglecting the ontological question, which neglect betrays a lack of self-criticism. He implies thereby that if German philosophy had been self-critical enough, if it had carried on its philosophical criticism far enough, it would necessarily have discovered its own involvement in the historical world. Marx's position is an attempt to radicalize the critical direction of German Idealism and claims, therefore, to be the most critical philosophy of all. However, in his quest for ontology, Marx immediately thinks of a kind of historical ontology. Thus, he assumes that being is ultimately to be found in the historical world.

4. *The Relation of Theory and Practice via Revolution*

4.1. Ultimately, Marx wants to *remind* philosophy of its factual (ontic) presuppositions, i.e., it is part of the historical world. Marx needs only a reminder, because these presuppositions can be discovered through self-criticism, in other words, through a philosophical negation of philosophy. However, problems develop: while maintaining that the factual presuppositions of philosophy can be discovered by self-criticism, – i.e., by intra-philosophical criticism, if only it is radical enough – he also says that we need a practical negation, an abolition of philosophy. This raises the question whether these two propositions are compatible.

Will Marx be able to discover a real connection between these two propositions or will he get stuck in their opposition? We alluded to this problem previously when we spoke of an attempt by Marx to "kill two birds with one stone". The problem is created by Marx's desire both to present a philosophical critique and also to exercise the preeminently practical turn of his philosophizing. This may be designated as the problem of theory and practice. This ambivalence is also reflected in the sentences we have already referred to quite often: "You cannot abolish philosophy without realizing it", and "You cannot realize philosophy without abolishing it". At first these statements seemed merely to complement each other, but now it becomes obvious that a tension exists between them. This duality comes through repeatedly. Take the following passage for example:

> The criticism of the *German philosophy of right and of the state* which was given its most logical, profound and complete expression by Hegel, is at once the critical analysis of the modern state and of the reality connected with it, and the definitive negation of all the past *forms of consciousness in German jurisprudence and politics,* whose most distinguished and most general expression, raised to the level of a *science,* is precisely the *speculative philosophy of right*[30].

4.2. This paragraph clearly shows Marx's admiration for Hegel, as he praises him for having provided the "most logical, profound and complete expression" of the German philosophy of right and of the state. But again he is trying to "kill two birds with one stone", for he says that his criticism of that German philosophy is at once the critical analysis of the modern state in a practical sense, but also that it is the definitive negation of all the former "*forms of consciousness in German jurisprudence and politics*", i.e., of the speculative philosophy of right. The artificiality of this union becomes obvious in the next sentence:

[30] *Ibid.,* p. 51.

If it was only Germany which could produce the speculative philosophy of right – this extravagant and abstract thought about the modern state, the reality of which remains in the beyond (even if this beyond is only across the Rhine) – the *German* representative of the modern state, on the contrary, which leaves out of account[31] the *real man* was itself only possible because, and to the extent that, the modern state itself leaves the *real man* out of account or only satisfies the *whole* man in an illusory way[32].

This contrived attempt to solve the complex problem of the relation between abstract theory (including abstract criticism) and practice, that is, practical involvement in the concrete world, by including abstractness in the practice of the modern state itself is simplistic, to say the least. The modern state and modern society abstract from or leave out of account the real man in their practice. Marx, thus, tries to relate theory and practice by pointing to this abstraction in the practice of the modern state. Although important aspects of man may indeed be neglected in the modern state, this is not the same as saying that there is a factual abstractness in the modern state. This appears to be a ploy to achieve a starting point for his attempt to "kill two birds with one stone".

4.3.   He develops this further in the following sentences:

In politics, Germans have *thought* what other nations have *done*. Germany has been their *theoretical consciousness*[33] [34].

The abstraction of German thought is equated with the abstraction of the real situation in the other modern states. Thus, German thought in its abstractness reflects the practice of the other states; however, as we have previously seen, this same thought is the most progressive aspect of German development and brings it on a par with the level of historical development of the other states. Accordingly, Marx can speak of Germany operating as their "theoretical conscience". This term is another attempt at fusing the theoretical and the practical, and as such it is hard to make sense of. For someone like Kant, it would have been a completely senseless term; for conscience, dealing as it does with morality, belongs to the sphere of practical reason and can hardly be combined with "theoretical".

4.4.   In the next paragraph Marx returns to the German situation as such, focusing especially on the practical:

---

[31] The German (abstrahiert von) literally reads, "abstracts from", instead of "leaves out of account", the real man.
[32] *Loc. cit.*
[33] "*Theoretical conscience*" is truer to the German text which uses the term "*Gewissen*".
[34] *Ibid.*, p. 51.

> As the determined adversary of the previous form of German political conscious-
> ness, the criticism of the speculative philosophy of right does not remain within
> its own sphere, but leads on to *tasks* which can only be solved by *means of
> practical activity*[35].

Here Marx is saying that the criticism of this significant German
political conscience (or "consciousness") as expressed in the German
philosophy of right has practical results. Thus, after a plodding,
theoretical dialectical beginning, Marx finally enunciates clearly his
practical concern and he expresses his awareness of being confronted
with a *practical* mission.

Nevertheless, Marx still maintains a theoretical philosophical starting
point; he remains a philosopher even while expressing his practical
concern. This is apparent also in the next paragraph:

> The question then arises: can Germany attain a practical activity *à la hauteur
> des principes* [on the same level as the principles – ed.]; that is to say, a
> revolution which will raise it not only to the *official level* of the modern
> nations, but to the *human level* which will be the immediate future of those
> nations[36].

In the preceding paragraph Marx turned to his practical aim. Now he
is going to elaborate that practical aim. However, he connects it with
principles which are to be established philosophically; this is what he
means by "*à la hauteur des principes*". They consist, in part, of the
principles of Hegel's philosophy of right (which is on a par with the
practice of the modern states) and in part, but especially, of the
principles which Marx claims to establish himself in his philosophical
criticism of Hegel's philosophy. The latter principles are supposed to
be an expression of the genuine human level which the immediate
future holds for the other nations. In this context, Marx raises the
question whether Germany can attain to a level of practical activity,
i.e., a revolution, which is in accordance with the high level of these
principles.

Notice that after having (only apparently) made clear the connection
between theory and practice, and after having evoked a future society
that is truly human, Marx for the first time uses the word *revolution*.
Heretofore he had only used such terms as "criticism", "negation" and
"abolition". Thus, the idea of revolution occurs in connection with his
concern to bring about a genuine human level in history and also in
connection with his labored attempt to relate theory and practice.

4.5.   But it seems that even Marx himself is aware that his theoretical
criticism does not easily fuse with his practical revolution.

---

[35] *Ibid.*, p. 52.
[36] *Ibid.*, p. 52.

It is clear that the arm of criticism [theoretical or philosophical criticism] cannot replace the criticism of arms [revolutionary criticism or war]. Material force can only be overthrown by material force . . . [37].

So Marx takes another approach: the next sentences are a series of revolutionary slogans that crackle like gunshots:

> . . . . but theory itself becomes a material force when it seizes the masses. Theory is capable of seizing the masses when it demonstrates *ad hominem*, and it demonstrates *ad hominem* as soon as it becomes radical. To be radical is to grasp things by the root. But for man the root is man himself[38].

How is this an attempt at integrating theory and practice?

Marx appeals to the demonstration *ad hominem*, or as it is usually called, the *argumentum ad hominem*. In the handbooks of logic it is described under the rubric of unsound arguments. This kind of argument is unsound because it does not prove, refute or show the truth/untruth of a certain statement or proposition, but instead moves away from the content of a given proposition or chain of propositions in order to address itself directly to the person. Given a person's moral beliefs or psychological attitudes, it asks him how he can sustain a particular statement. The tenability of the content of a certain proposition or chain of propositions is no longer at stake here, but merely certain non-logical factors. Note that we said *non*-logical factors, not *il*logical factors; for, every argument usually has non-logical aspects. Only when an argument fails as a logical argument, moving *away from* the logically testable content of a proposition *to* these non-logical aspects, can it be called *ad hominem*.

When Marx says that "Theory is capable of seizing the masses when it demonstrates *ad hominem*", he is making demagogical use of this fallacious type of argument. But, evidently, he is not really concerned with demonstrating the logical truth or untruth of a statement. He is instead concerned with the violent, revolutionary conversion of man and masses of men. Without attempting to make any judgements regarding the necessity of such a conversion, we are still led to aks: why present it in the guise of a logical argument? Marx seems to be trying to maintain the appearance that he as a philosopher is just proposing a radical *theory*. This is not an entirely new procedure, for Hegel employed a similar ruse. In order to demonstrate how reality and thought fuse with each other Hegel used "dialectical logic", which he defended as a radicalization of sound theoretical thought. Marx employs another ruse – the *argumentum ad hominem* – for a similar goal. This goal, like Hegel's, is also a kind of identity of thought and

---

[37] *Ibid.*, p. 52.
[38] *Loc. cit.*

being, for he wants to attribute to theory the power to grasp man in the depths of his being, in his roots.

4.6.   This reference to man's root – "But for man the root is man himself" is another statement of Marx's humanism. It is akin to that statement we analysed previously where Marx spoke of man revolving about himself as his own true sun. We said at that time, the latter statement could not be taken as a real theoretical statement – not even by Marx's own standards. But in this case, Marx introduces his statement in the context of a discussion on the function of theory, thereby suggesting that this is indeed a theoretical statement. In fact, he continues with the words, "What proves beyond doubt . . .", imparting thereby the appearance of a logical argument. This (apparent) argument culminates in the statement that *"man is the supreme being for man"*, thus harking back to the opening sentence of the essay. However, like the previous statement of his humanism, it is not the conclusion of an argument, but just another confession or credo.

The next sentence is a similar supra- or fore-theoretical statement in the guise of a theoretical argument:

> It ends, therefore, with the *categorical imperative to overthrow all those conditions* in which man is an abased, enslaved, abandoned, contemptible being – conditions which can hardly be better described than in the exclamation of a Frenchman on the occasion of a proposed tax upon dogs: "Wretched dogs! They want to treat you like men!"[39]

Marx is here deliberately alluding to the categorical imperative of Kant, to whom it represented the core of our morality, the symbol of man's highest dignity. It is the "ought" that is unconditionally valid, that holds under any circumstances. Marx alludes to this Kantian idea in the context of his humanistic concern for man; his doctrine that "man is the supreme being for man" implies this categorical imperative "to overthrow all those conditions . . .". The former doctrine is his starting point (although he does not present it as such, but as an end or conclusion) and the latter imperative is the ultimate consequence of that starting point. Note how Marx's humanistic doctrine and its implied categorical imperative lead to a practical discrimination between men. For this overthrowal of "conditions" involves people, and these people – those whom Marx calls the oppressors – become the victims of this overthrow. Nor are we reading this into the text: we have only to remember Marx's previous allusion to "hand to hand" combat. Of course, one might counter that this discrimination, in which some men become victims, is only a temporary interlude after which the humanistic doctrine of man will again become operative. However, the categorical imperative which leads to this discriminatory action is not just a

[39] *Ibid.*, p. 52.

57

consequence of a specific argument, but functions as a standard by which to discern true humanity.

Recapitulating: the categorical imperative is the *prescriptive* statement that derives from the universal *descriptive* statement that man is his own supreme being, for this description of man leads to the inference that those conditions inimical to this ideal have to be overthrown. Thus, it sets up a pre-theoretical commitment *not to man as such, but to a certain ideal type of man*. So it seems that in this so-called descriptive theory which Marx presents certain normative views are implied.

This also casts a different light on Marx's position on religion; for his interpretation of religion as just an out-dated illusion was presented as a purely descriptive discovery. But now that we have seen that his way of arguing implies and presupposes certain normative views of his own, namely, that man is his own supreme being, we are forced to re-evaluate his claim that his opposition is a theoretical description.

4.7. Having introduced the idea of a radical revolution, Marx begins his elaboration of that idea by first touching on "a major difficulty", which is its need for a *passive* element, a *material* basis. Theory thus still predominates; it maintains the initiative; it is active. Or as Marx puts it:

> It is not enough that thought should seek to realize itself; reality must also strive towards thought[40].

When he introduces this passive, material basis it is only as an element within the context of theory; but it is, nevertheless, a new element.

Until now this new element appeared mainly as that which presented resistance to philosophy's becoming worldly; in the process of becoming worldly or practical, it encounters a material reality that resists it. But now Marx says that the revolutionary practice, which is the end of the process by which philosophy becomes worldly, needs passivity as a basis on which to operate or as an element within which to operate. Underlying this new emphasis of Marx is a shift in attention to a different aspect of man. As long as he was dealing with the development of philosophical criticism, Marx focused on man as an active being, as a being with will and with the energy to exercise that will in creative acts. The most striking expression of this active, creative side of human being is philosophy becoming will or practical energy. Philosophy itself has to end in revolutionary energy. But having said that, Marx now goes on to say that man is also a being with needs:

> Theory is only realized in a people so far as it fulfills the needs of the people[41].

We have discussed this concept of "needs" before. As we have pointed

[40] *Ibid.*, p. 54.
[41] *Ibid.*, p. 53.

out, this concept obviously implies that man is dependent on something outside of himself. But what kind of needs does Marx have in mind? Marx points us to civil society and the state for the answer:

> Will there correspond to the monstrous discrepancy between the demands of German thought and the answers of German reality a similar discrepancy between civil society and the state, and within civil society itself?[42]

Marx previously said that first we have to criticize the philosophy of right and of the state and then those realities themselves; here he has come to those realities: civil society and the state. But those realities appear first of all as a passive element. Within this passive element or material basis, Marx goes on to say, there has to be a discrepancy similar to the one he pointed out between the demands of German thought and the answers of German reality. The latter discrepancy was a necessary presupposition for radical revolution. Since the radical revolution presupposes a passive element, this discrepancy must be inherent also in this passive element. Marx thus posits this discrepancy not first of all between civil society and the state but also and especially within civil society itself.

It may be fruitful at this point to remind ourselves of our earlier discussion of Hegel's idea of civil society and the state. The main feature of that civil society for both Hegel and Marx is that it is economically qualified; it is society orientated to the acquisition of goods. According to Hegel, this civil society had to be superseded by the state as the objective form of the moral idea. Whereas, in Marx it is precisely within civil society itself that real historical progress has to be made. The state for Marx is that abstract monster which is responsible for the terrible discrepancy within civil society which has made man "an abased, enslaved, abandoned, contemptible being". The need for and the meaning of a radical revolution are thus to be found primarily within civil society. Therefore, Marx's question regarding the presence of that discrepancy in German society is vital to him, for it is the necessary condition for revolution. If a revolution requires a material basis or passive element, and if that basis is civil society and if civil society is an organization of needs, then the revolution must be first of all a revolution of radical needs. This is the conclusion that Marx comes to:

> A radical revolution can only be a revolution of radical needs, for which the conditions and the breeding ground appear to be lacking[43].

In our time of conspicuous consumption and everything else that is associated with an affluent society, this may sound very appealing,

[42] *Ibid.*, p. 53.
[43] *Ibid.*, p. 54.

and to a certain extent, we can perhaps agree with Marx, a revolution requires a revolution of our needs. But for Marx, the term "radical" remains within the framework of an economically qualified society. In other words, the radicalization and humanization of needs does not pass beyond those economic limits for him.

4.8.   This emphasis on the material basis in an economical sense is our first engagement with Marx's concept of historical materialism. We immediately detect a certain difficulty within this conception. When we focus on the expression, "revolution of radical needs", we are faced with an enigma. For since the organization of needs within civil society occurs as the passive element, what is the source of the revolutionary dynamic? Needs present themselves to us, they urge themselves upon us and more or less determine their own course. Would this not lead to a wait and see attitude rather than a revolution?

On the other hand, if instead of emphasizing the term "needs", we emphasize the term "revolution", i.e., revolution as active interference, then the emphasis also falls on "historical" in historical materialism. Then it is man who is the active power in history, who has to interfere actively in his reality. This emphasis becomes difficult to reconcile with the idea of passivity and of needs that urge themselves upon us. If we wish to maintain the former active emphasis, then we have to reinterpret needs to mean willfull drives. Then also "revolution of radical needs" comes to mean a revolution against certain dominant willfull drives in society. These drives that Marx wishes to combat are the strivings of the dominant class. Here we seem to have unearthed the class struggle. However, either of our two interpretations is possible; the point we wish to make is that the expression "revolution of radical needs" is ambiguous.

We have as yet left Marx's question unanswered: can Germany rise to the historical level necessary for revolution? We have thus far followed Marx as he pointed out major obstacles. Before we follow him to his proposed solutions, let us first briefly summarize what has been said.

> 1) Marx advocates a *radical* revolution which will raise Germany to a human level.
> 2) This revolution requires a passive element, a material basis, which is civil society as economically qualified.
> 3) Such a revolution presupposes discrepancies.
> 4) A radical revolution presupposes radical discrepancies.
> 5) This radical discrepancy is found in the passive element, the material basis; thus, revolution is a revolution of radical needs.

4.9.   Marx's argument to this point still leaves a major difficulty untouched: the question whether the conditions for radical revolution exist in the material basis, that is, in the civil society of Germany. Here

Germany fails the test; nowhere is the passivity of this passive element as great as in Germany.

> But if Germany accompanied the development of the modern nations only through the abstract activity of thought, without taking an active part in the real struggles of this development, it has also experienced the *pains* of this development without sharing in its pleasures and partial satisfactions. The abstract activity on one side has its counterpart in the abstract suffering on the other[44].

In its abstract thought, Germany has attained a historical level corresponding to the level of abstract suffering of other nations. Marx uses a play on the word "abstract" in order to bring out a contrast: in the second sense, it refers to general suffering at the passive, i.e., sociopolitical level, and in the first sense, to philosophical activity.

Marx goes on to describe the political situation in Germany. He finds it so deplorable; the only way out is a radical revolution which will remove the whole thoroughly defective system. A partial revolution which would leave the pillars standing is only a utopian dream; it would not emancipate Germany from this deplorable situation. A partial revolution would be like pouring new wine into old wine skins. Of course, this raises the question why a radical revolution would be any less of a utopian dream.

4.10. Marx has not excluded the possibility that in some other countries a genuine human level might be attained by a partial revolution, such as a merely or mainly *political* revolution. For example, general availability of money or culture to everyone can create an adequate human level which would make a radical revolution unnecessary. However, a necessary condition for even such a partial revolution is that a section of civil society emancipate first itself and then society in general. Any revolution, even a partial one, must start from the material basis, civil society. For a partial revolution to occur certain conditions must first exist.

First, in order for a certain class to emancipate society in general all the rest of that society must be in the same situation as this leading class.

Second, this class must be able to generate enthusiasm that will cause the rest of society to identify with it. Thus, revolutionary emotion or energy plays a vital role in the making of a revolution.

And third, one class must be presented as a general obstacle and oppressor to the whole society.

In the third point, a *general* division into two classes is introduced with an *irreducible* opposition between them. The division is general because civil society represents the whole, the most general category

---

[44] *Ibid.*, p. 54.

for Marx. The opposition is irreducible, again, because it occurs within the material basis, civil society, which is a basic common denominator. In the process, the negative class, which concentrates in itself all the evils and crimes of society, and the liberating class, as the negation of the negation, both take on a strong moral coloration. The result is a general and irreducible division of civil society into the good and the bad guys.

The all-pervasiveness of Marx's dialectical method is quite obvious here. Civil society functions as a kind of dialectical unity in which *one* class assumes a *general* mission. However, in order to perform that mission, this class has to *presuppose* the existence of *another* class. Thus, his dialectical method causes Marx to split up his ultimate, material basis. He then seems to unite the two classes dialectically in a unity of opposites by giving each a general function. So we see how Marx grafts his idea of the historical power struggle into the supposed universality of the dialectical scheme. Further, this historical power struggle has its main basis and field of operation in the economic area; and finally, the main categories (like negativity, struggle, etc.) suddenly get a strong moral coloration.

Examining the German situation once more, Marx concludes that the conditions for a partial or political revolution do not exist; for, the generosity of spirit necessary to cause a class to identify with the popular mind or to create a general sentiment does not exist,

> "Even the *moral sentiment of the German middle class* has no other basis than the consciousness of being the representative of the narrow and limited mediocrity of all the other classes"[45].

Marx thus concludes that it is precisely the deadness, the complete impossibility of the German situation that makes it ripe for a complete revolution,

> "In France it is enough to be something in order to desire to be everything. In Germany no one has the right to be anything without first renouncing everything. In France partial emancipation is a basis for complete emancipation. In Germany complete emancipation is a *conditio sine qua non* for any partial emancipation. In France it is the reality, in Germany the impossibility, of a progressive emancipation which must give birth to complete liberty"[46].

In other words, conditions in France make a partial or political revolution viable, but the entirely adverse conditions in Germany make a radical revolution the only possibility. Thus, Marx has led us to the question:

> "Where is there, then, a *real* possibility of emancipation in Germany?"[47]

[45] *Ibid.*, pp. 56, 57.
[46] *Ibid.*, p. 57.
[47] *Ibid.*, p. 58.

We quote his reply in full:

> "*This is our reply.* A class must be formed which has *radical chains*, a class in civil society which is not a class of civil society, a class which is the dissolution of all classes, a sphere of society which has a universal character because its sufferings are universal, and which does not claim a *particular redress* because the wrong which is done to it is not a *particular wrong* but *wrong in general.* There must be formed a sphere of society which claims no *traditional* status but only a human status, a sphere which is not opposed to particular consequences but is totally opposed to the assumptions of the German political system; a sphere, finally, which cannot emancipate itself without emancipating itself from all the other spheres of society, without, therefore, emancipating all these other spheres, which is, in short, a *total loss* of humanity and which can only redeem itself by a *total redemption of humanity.* This dissolution of society, as a particular class, is the *proletariat*"[48].

The tradition behind the term "redeem" is the Jewish notion of the substitutionary suffering of the Jews for the sake of mankind. However, in the context of Marx's interpretation of the loss and redemption of humanity it loses its Judeo-Christian content and becomes part of his dialectical scheme.

There is a continuity between this view of human self-redemption and the humanistic credo that we examined at the beginning: man revolves around himself "as his own true sun". However, beside this continuity between starting point and conclusion, we can also detect a discontinuity: while the starting point is optimistic, the conclusion is pessimistic, even tragic, Marx evokes a "total loss of humanity"; the concomitant "total redemption" is in no way a Christian concept. It is the desperate hope of alienated man trying to find comfort only in himself – as "his own true sun".

4.11. Has Marx presented a real solution to his own major problem? When he speaks of the formation of the proletariat, he says: "A class *must* be formed . . ."; whereas, earlier he based himself on the *given* situation in Germany. Is this development (radical emancipation) a must in the material sense (either mechanical or organic), as he seems to say in the following sentence:

> "In Germany, on the contrary, where practical life is as little intellectual as intellectual life is practical, no class of civil society feels the need for, or the ability to achieve, a general emancipation, until it is forced to it by its *immediate* situation, by *material* necessity and by its *fetters themselves*"[49].

Or does this development depend upon a willful intervention of a class which has to be formed? Is the proletariat a "mass resulting from the disintegration of society" or does it form itself? Both of these tendencies are present in one sentence, when Marx says:

[48] *Ibid.*, p. 58.
[49] *Ibid.*, p. 58.

> "When the proletariat announces the *dissolution of the existing social order,*
> it only declares the *secret of its own existence,* for it *is* the *effective* dissolution
> of this order"[50].

The proletariat comes into being with the dissolution of the existing
order; in announcing its dissolution, it announces its own existence. At
the same time, however, it is supposed to be the *effective* dissolution
of this order. In order to link these two disparate tendencies he uses
the term "secret". This is the secret of Marx's history. It requires a
seer, a prophet to reveal this "secret" to the masses.

Here, for the first time in the history of thought, *negation* (as a
component of the theoretical dialectic) is presented as a universal
praxis, or as the practice of the proletariat in its universal function.
When he speaks of the "loss of humanity", Marx is speaking of the
proletariat as the negation of all classes. It had never entered Hegel's
mind to conceive of dialectic in this way: to embody the negation in a
real class. Thus, the difficult and laborious course of Marx's thought was
to give the theoretical term "negation" a practical meaning. Although
we have to qualify this course as one of philosophical mystification,
and although the embodiment of the negation in a real "class" should
be considered a revolutionary mystification, this does not detract from
the historical import of the turn Marx gives here to the idea of "negation".

4.12. What has happened to the status of philosophy now that the
theoretical has become embodied in a real class? Has civil society or the
material structure displaced philosophy? Philosophy has not been
abolished, as Marx points out:

> Just as philosophy finds its *material* weapon in the proletariat, so the proletariat
> finds its *intellectual* weapons in philosophy. And once the lightning of thought
> has penetrated deeply into this virgin soil of the people, the *Germans* will
> emancipate themselves and become *men*[51].

Philosophy thus serves as a kind of temporary preparation for the
final purpose. As we saw earlier, philosophy is in the service of history.
And the real dynamic of history, its heart, is the rising proletariat.
Philosophy functions only as the head.

> *Philosophy* is the *head* of this emancipation and the *proletariat* is its *heart*[52].

However, this does not mean that philosophy no longer plays a decisive
role. It preserves a universal purport as well; as the "lightning of
thought", it remains the ultimate revealer and interpreter of the secret

---

[50] *Ibid.,* pp. 58, 59.
[51] *Ibid.,* p. 59.
[52] *Ibid.,* p. 59.

of history. The proletariat as the heart of history can only become aware of its universal role by listening to its head – philosophy.

A certain discord or tension persists to the end in Marx's conception. Philosophy as the revealer, as the *ad hominem* demonstration, has become so powerless that it needs the material support (force) of the proletarian activists. On the other hand, the practical power of the proletariat is so inadequate that it cannot do without the directives provided by philosophy.

CHAPTER V

Marx's Economic & Philosophic Manuscripts

1. *Introduction*

Before we get into the *Economic and Philosophic Manuscripts* we should make a few transitional remarks. In the last essay, we noticed how Marx emphasized the significance of the material basis as a condition for a radical and genuinely human revolution. He located this basis in civil society which was economically qualified. In the *Economic and Philosophic Manuscripts* Marx pursues this line further in the development of his thought. Especially two concepts are important: labor and money. One has only to glance at the titles of the various essays to confirm this. Labor and money are the two main pivotal points on which his ideas on the material basis can obtain leverage.

First, let us consider the two-fold adjective in the titel: "Economic" and "Philosophic". Recall that in his first essay Marx described the material basis as a passive element. In the subsequent essays this passive element becomes less and less passive and also less and less of an element. For it is in this so-called passive sphere that real, authentic *praxis* has to be located. And rather than being simply an element in which we live, like the air we breathe, it becomes more like a battle field or a theater of war. This is especially true as the productive activity of the *laborer*, with the devaluation of both the laborer and his labor, become the key phenomenon for Marx. He wants to point out that in this passive sphere the capitalist becomes the incarnation of inauthentic humanity: he possesses an inauthentic, alien power because it is *not* founded on his own productive activity or labor, all he does is sit about collecting profits and raking in rent.

Secondly, besides being the arena where authentic and inauthentic praxis meet head-on, the economic situation is also seen as an objective counterpart to a theoretical course of thought. This accounts for the second adjective in *Economic and Philosophic Manuscripts*. The theoretical course of thought poses certain ideal demands to which certain immanent necessities in the objective field of the economic situation are supposed to correspond. This makes for a strange but interesting combination.

In the first instance, where the emphasis is on the material basis as a real basis also for theoretical thought, activity is not determined at all, it itself is the main determining factor. But in the second instance, where this material basis becomes merely an object of philosophical thought, labor and the relationships of productivity appear as a process that can be analysed in terms of objective necessity. To put it differently, in the first case, philosophic thought seems to be dependent upon the primary activity that occurs in the economic situation, while in the second case, philosophy seems to be ahead of the situation claiming to prescribe certain ideal demands for the situation and evaluating it by such ideal philosophic standards. One gets the impression that, in the first case, philosophy has but to derive its program of action from the primary and given activity of the laborer himself: thus philosophy is secondary to the proletariat, in fact, the laborer in his labor prescribes the form of philosophy. In the second case, where philosophy is supposed to frame a program for action, dialectics as developed by Hegel is the instrument by which theoretical demands, constructions and programs for action are formulated. Thus, Marx adopted dialectics in its universal prescriptive function from Hegel, borrowing such key notions as alienation, externalization and objectification. These preliminary remarks will become clearer as we consider specific passages in the *Economic and Philosophic Manuscripts*.

2. *Estranged Labor*

2.1.   The first of the *Manuscripts* we shall consider is the one entitled "Estranged Labor". And the first thing we wish to take note of is the point that Marx makes of its being empirical.

> We proceed from an economic fact *of the present*[1].

His analysis proceeds from a factual situation. He contrasts this starting point with the abstract speculations and fictions of the leading contemporary economists, which he has referred to in the preceding paragraph.

The rest of the paragraph quoted from reads:

> The worker becomes all the poorer the more wealth he produces, the more his production increases in power and size. The worker becomes an even cheaper commodity the more commodities he creates. With the *increasing value* of the world of things proceeds in direct proportion the *devaluation* of the world of men. Labor produces not only commodities: it produces itself and the worker as a *commodity* – and this in the same general proportion in which it produces commodities[2].

[1] Dirk J. Struik, transl., *The Economic & Philosophic Manuscripts of 1844*, p. 107. All quotes are from this edition unless otherwise indicated.
[2] *Ibid.*, p. 107.

This is a summary of what he has said more elaborately in preceding sections which were an analysis of certain existing, general prevalent conditions of production. The term "conditions of production" is an important term for Marx and becomes even more important in his development; it contrasts with the term "powers of production". These general conditions of production are determined, on the one hand, by their being owned and organized for profit by the capitalist, and on the other hand, by the capitalists need for and use of labor power. These existing conditions as such form a more or less passive element from which Marx has to start in order to make his criticism effective. In fact, recalling the relationship he posited earlier between the passive economic element and revolution, we may say that even the revolution depends on it.

Within the existing conditions of production, Marx evaluates the product of labor almost exclusively in economic terms. The product of labor is no longer a piece of self-realization in which the laborer recognizes himself; or, to use abstract Hegelian terms, also favored by Marx himself, there is no longer only a negative antithesis between the laborer's production and his real product. In fact, conditions are such that even labor itself, that is, the producing activity itself, is bound to make a commodity both of itself and of its subject, the laborer: "Labor produces not only commodities: it produces itself and the worker as a *commodity* . . . ". Marx's main concern is, thus, the devaluation of the subject and of his authentic producing activity. This activity has to ultimately and inalienably remain the laborer's own. Although Marx is attempting to discover possibilities toward a humanizing of the situation, he himself also approaches the activity of the human subject from the viewpoint of economic production.

2.2.   There are two misleading oversimplifications we should forestall. The devaluation of the laborer and his labor is not simply a matter of the preponderance of the product or commodity as such. Nor does all evil reside in the other subjects, the capitalists. Marx does not just want to take a moral stance and point an accusing finger at the capitalists, suggesting that if only they were done away with all would be well. Such an interpretation would be doing an injustice to Marx's seriousness. Marx wants to analyse the situation, not just moralize about it. He wants to see that situation as a complex whole of which the capitalist is only a component. It is the situation as a whole that suffers from internal contradictions. Nevertheless, the terms that Marx uses in describing the situation do sometimes have a strong moral flavor. But it is not Marx's intention to stay at the level of moral denunciation. Marx wants to point out that the situation of production, the material basis, must itself be broken through, surpassed.

2.3.   One of the evils inherent in the material basis, as Marx points out elsewhere, is the fact of the division of labor. The division of labor robs the laborer of the chance to recognize and experience himself as a whole or total man because he must abandon the opportunity to unfold his selfhood in its full freedom and variety. Instead, he is tied to the mechanical character of the labor process brought about by the division of labor. There are actually two ideas involved here which reside together in an uncomfortable tension; in fact, the tension proceeds from a basic polarity in Marx's thought. The two ideas are that of *self-production*, i.e., man producing himself as man, and that of *self-movement* or *automation*.

2.4.   The idea of free self-production is fundamental to man's self-interpretation and has long been such an idea in the history of Western philosophy. Spinoza expressed the same idea in his conception of God as an all-comprehensive subject. As *causa sui* God is free from all external causal influence; He is self-producing. Descartes had said that in order to be sure of one's own existence, one must first *make* sure *that* and *how* one exists. This same quest can be discerned in Hegel's impressive attempt to disclose the development of mind. To Hegel the subject is its own autonomous assignment; it must realize itself. Over against this subject stands a world of automatic processes. This "over against" involves a dualism which allows no resolution or real integration. Yet, each presupposes the other, needs the other and must meet the other. Marx also adopts this framework. As we have seen earlier, Hegel included negation, conflict and alienation as necessary factors within the process by which subjective mind produces itself. In its free self-producing power subjective mind, finally, overcomes all the conflicts, negation and alienation. We also pointed out that to Marx this construction was an abstract and unreal solution. He felt that certain real tensions and conflicts were either neglected or underestimated in Hegel's construction. He wanted to intensify the tensions, to take them more seriously. However, he continues to come to grips with these tensions using the same categories as Hegel. Other philosophers employed the theme of a free self-producing subject in a moralistic context, but Marx wants to use it in the context of the real historical and economic tensions of the Industrial Revolution. It is questionable how well a subject, primarily conceived of as free self-production, can manage in a world which stands over against it and which is basically conceived of as mechanical, automatic processes.

2.5.   Marx makes deliberate use of some of these Hegelian categories in order to provide a framework for the complex situation he wishes to describe. For he wishes to avoid the simplification that we have pointed out earlier. Consider the following passage:

> This fact expresses merely that the object which labor produces – labor's product – confronts it as *something alien*, as a *power independent* of the producer. The

product of labor is labor which has been embodied in an object, which has become material: it is the *objectification* of labor. Labor's realization is its objectification. In the sphere of political economy this realization of labor appears as *loss of realization* for the worker; objectification as *loss of the object* and *bondage to it*; appropriation as *estrangement*, as *alienation*[3].

The first Hegelian category that we detect in this passage is the concept of "something alien", which he ascribes to the object. In this connection, the word used in the German for object is significant: *"Gegenstand"*, which literally means "contrary to or standing over against". Thus, the original makes it more clear that there is *opposition* involved. John Dewey makes a similar point when he observes that an object is first of all a thing that objects. In this case, the alien being of the *"Gegenstand"* is the alien being of the product. The second category is that of "objectification": *"Vergegenständlichung"* – the process of becoming an object. When labor as a productive activity becomes embodied in a product, it too becomes a product, an object. For the third category we could coin the word "de-realization", *"Entwirklichung"*, which Struik translates with "the loss of realization". The last category we wish to point out is that of "alienation"; Struik adds the word "estrangement". The German term is *"Entäusserung"*, a literal rendering into English would be "making external to oneself" or "externalize", which adequately captures what Hegel and Marx usually mean by the term. All four of these key notions presuppose the dualistic scheme of the world that we referred to earlier: a more or less internal subject world in which the subject can freely realize and produce itself over against the external object world of fixed things and processes.

2.6.   Notice the close connection that Marx posits between "labor's realization" and "objectification". He almost identifies the two: "Labor's realization is its objectification". This near-identification is self-evident for Marx and is, as such, not a bad thing. But it is related to the dualistic scheme which we have pointed out. In that scheme, the term "real" is attributed to what is visible and tangible – a physical and material thing; it is "over there", over against me, in the world of objects or "Gegenstände". In other words, that which I conceive within myself, or more generally, that which I produce out of myself, in order to become really real, has to make a transition to that objective outer world which is the real world. However, because that objective world is an "other" world, "over against" myself, the transition necessarily implies some degree of alienation. Nevertheless, because the object or product as such remains *my* product, it at the same time must stay in contact with me. So Marx's criticism does not start at this point: for him, too, the alienation of the product is, to some extent,

[3] *Ibid.*, p. 108.

inevitable as it makes the transition from my subjective world to the real, objective world.

Marx's real criticism begins with the line: "In the sphere of political economy this realization of labor appears as *loss of realization* for the worker ... ". This is actually a succinct statement of three different points, corresponding to the triadic scheme of dialectics: thesis, antithesis, synthesis. Or to use more Hegelian terms: a position or affirmation, its negation and finally a negation of the negation which supersedes the opposition between the preceding two. The "realization of labor" corresponds to the thesis or affirmation; "objectification" to the antithesis or negation; and "appropriation" to the synthesis or the negation of the negation.

The thesis, or the "realization of labor", involves the desire of the laborer as a subject to realize and affirm himself in his labor activity. Thus, labor posits itself; or to put it another way, the laborer posits himself. German Idealism framed the thesis differently. Its thesis did not include an explicit reference to the object or product, but involved only the self-positing of the subject. For example, Fichte's basic proposition was: "The self posits itself", which does not contain any reference to an object. Whereas, in Marx, this explicit reference to the object is presupposed in the statement that the realization of labor is objectification. For Marx, the object world has gained importance. Thus, although he adopts the Idealist scheme, Marx introduces a considerable change.

How does Marx, now, apply this adopted but altered scheme in his criticism of the present situation? Marx states as a critique that the self-realization of the laborer, the affirmation or thesis, which ought to be a positive activity, turns out in fact to be a loss of realization or "de-realization", in other words, a negative situation. He expresses this very concretely, when he says in the next paragraph: "So much does labor's realization appear as loss of realization that the worker loses realization to the point of starving to death". Due to the existing conditions of production, the very first *necessary* realization has become an *impossible* one.

The antithesis, called "objectification", he describes as a "loss of the object and bondage to it". Although it is "labor which has been embodied in an object and turned into a physical thing", its physical status also implies a certain distance. For the objective product assumes a certain independence over against the producing activity.

Again we can detect a difference between Marx's view of the antithesis and that of German Idealism. In Fichte, whose thesis was "the self posits itself", a certain non-self appears over against the self-identity of the self in the thesis; this non-self is the antithesis. Similarly, in

71

Hegel, who described the thesis as "mind-in-its-self-affirmation", the antithesis becomes "mind-in-its-being-something-else".

In both Marx and the Idealists the antithesis contains reference to the self or mind that posits itself. However, to describe the objective, material world simply as "non-self" or "non-mind" is no longer adequate for Marx. For, the objective world-in-its-being-there, as a given, urges itself upon us and has to be recognized and accepted by our self or mind. But it does not as such contain an immediate reference to the self or mind; it simply happens to be there. It is for this reason that the objective world already appeared in Marx's thesis, i.e., in the realization of labor. However, Marx maintains a separate category for the objective world because he wishes to emphasize the independence of the world over against the self. In the first category the world is considered only in respect to the self-realization of the laborer. It is conceived of as an immediate expression of the active subject. Although this self-realization cannot be accomplished without objectification, a new element appears with this objectification; accordingly, objectification must be maintained as a separate category.

When he applies this concept of objectification to the present situation, Marx says that it has come to mean a loss of the object, even a servitude and bondage to the object. So it seems that objectification has to occur in such a way that the object is preserved or maintained in relation to the subject, the laborer. Marx's starting point is the active, productive laborer. The laborer must keep his role as initiator; he has the right to manipulate the world of objects and to stamp that world with the sign of his free productivity and mastery. In the present situation the opposite happens:

> So much does objectification appear as loss of the object that the worker is robbed of the object most necessary not only for his life but for his work. Indeed, labor itself becomes an object which he can obtain only with the greatest effort and with the most irregular interruptions[4].

The equivalent of the Idealist synthesis or the negation of the negation is "appropriation" in Marx's terms. Here, that which as object stood over against the self (as subjective laborer, i.e., in its self-realization) is included in the self again; in other words, it is appropriated by the subject. Or to use an interesting play on words, it becomes a *property* of the subject.

2.7. When Marx brings this concept of appropriation to bear on the contemporary situation, he observes that what ought to be the final reconciliation of opposites turns out to be alienation or estrangement:

[4] *Ibid.*, p. 108.

"So much does the appropriation of the object appear as estrangement that the more objects the worker produces the less he can possess and the more he falls under the sway of his product, capital"[5].

Because Marx began by allowing the object or product a greater degree of independence over against the productive activity of the subject, his idea of appropriation is more determined by a concept of possession than is that of the German Idealists. The latter never allowed the object an independent status, accordingly, to them, appropriation (synthesis, negation of the negation) meant primarily the emergence of the objective product as a real property of the subject as such, as a feature of its subjective activity. In German Idealism, especially in Hegel, alienation first of all means self-alienation. Its starting point is independent mind. Whatever conflicts or oppositions this mind experiences are really only moments of self-alienation in its own self-development. Thus, Hegel could say that negation or antithesis is the mind becoming something else. It is this same mind, or self (subject) that overcomes this becoming-something-else in order to assimilate it into its own complete being. In Marx, however, as Struik points out in an explanatory note, the legal-commercial connotations of the term alienation (German: *Entfremdung*) come to the fore[6]. However, the difference between Marx and the Idealists is mainly one of emphasis, Marx concentrating mainly on the object "over there".

But Marx is not content to rest there; now he shifts his focus to "the *act of production*, within the *producing activity*, itself"[7]. This shift allies Marx more closely to the Idealistic conception of self-alienation. Alienation does not first appear in the relationship between subject and object, but it is already present in the act of production itself – "the alienation of activity and the activity of alienation"[8]. Marx considers this to be the deepest, most basic level of alienation; this is alienation in its original form.

Genuine labor, according to Marx, has to be truly productive labor, labor in which human freedom can express itself directly. This presupposes a conception of human freedom as self-affirmation.

[5] *Ibid.*, p. 108.
[6] *Ibid.*, p. 59. "The ordinary dictionary meanings for *entfremden* are "to estrange", "to alienate", but in the present volume "estrange" has always been used. The reason is not only that "alienate" was needed for *entäussern*, but also that *entfremden* is only equivalent to "alienate" in *one* sense of the English word – in the sense in which we speak of two people being "alienated", or of someone's affections being "alienated". *Entfremden* has not the legal-commercial undertones of "alienate", and would not be used, for instance, to describe a transfer of property. Hence, despite the fact that translators of Marx have often rendered *entfremdet* as "alienated", "estranged" seems better, especially as Marx does also use *entäussert*, which *is* the equivalent of "alienated" in its legal-commercial sense".
[7] *Ibid.*, p. 110.
[8] *Ibid.*, p. 110.

What, then, constitutes the alienation of labor?
First, the fact that labor is *external* to the worker, i.e., it does not belong to his essential being; that in his work, therefore, he does not affirm himself but denies himself ... [9].

Using this concept as a basis, Marx combats primarily two tendencies. First of all, he laments the devaluation of labor to where it serves merely as a *means*:

His labor is therefore not voluntary, but coerced; it is *forced labor*. It is therefore not the satisfaction of a need; it is merely a *means* to satisfy needs external to it [10].

As a mere means or *medium*, labor is no longer the *immediate* expression of the laborer's self-affirmation. In its contemporary alienation, it stands in between the productive selfhood of the laborer and something that is external to this self-affirmation. This something external to self-affirmation is the satisfaction of certain needs. Apparently, Marx has in mind such "needs" as the "need" for competition, for making profit, for gaining private property and the like. Thus, labor becomes a means toward an external end.

Secondly, on the basis of this ideal of labor as an immediate expression of self-affirmation, Marx condemns the situation that leads to the laborer's being employed by *others*:

Lastly, the external character of labor for the worker appears in the fact that it is not his own, but someone else's, that it does not belong to him, that in it he belongs, not to himself, but to another [11].

This involves a shift in Marx's view of labor. Earlier he viewed labor as something in which a person can express, affirm or realize himself, where one can *be* himself,; now he views it as something that can be *possessed*. As a result, a certain vacillation or ambiguity is introduced in the use of his concept of alienation. This ambiguity, as we shall see, also influences his idea of communism.

2.8. Having considered the laborer's alienation from the object or product and his alienation from the act of production, Marx now goes on to discern a third form of alienation: man's alienation from his species-being.

Man is a species being, not only because in practice and in theory he adopts the species as his object (his own as well as those of other things), but – and this is only another way of expressing it – also because he treats himself as the actual, living species; because he treats himself as a *universal* and therefore a free being [12].

[9] *Ibid.*, p. 110.
[10] *Ibid.*, p. 110-111.
[11] *Ibid.*, p. 111.
[12] *Ibid.*, p. 112.

This form of alienation reduces man to a more or less atomistic individual. Marx is here concerned with asserting man's communal nature; mankind is a community.

In connection with this concern Marx uses the term "species" or "*Gattung*" in German. Originally, this term was a biological one; Aristotle already used it in this sense. Although it would not be fair to Marx to limit his meaning strictly to this biological sense, nevertheless, its use does suggest a more or less naturalistic basis. This naturalistic tendency comes out even more strongly when we read:

> That man's physical and spiritual life is linked to nature means simply that nature is linked to itself, for man is a part of nature[13].

However, his is not a purely naturalistic view, for he relates his notion of mankind as a community to man's ability to objectify (*Vergegenständlichung*), i.e., to set something over against thought as an object. In characterizing human consciousness by its ability to objectify, Marx joins with Feuerbach. To make certain things an object is typical of man's abstract theoretical reasoning. The term "*Gegenstand*" originates in the theoretical sphere of thought. A certain thing or event becomes an object when it is artificially isolated and distantiated in order to better distinguish certain features. It is true that Marx does combat certain absolutized theoretical abstractions; he views them as a form of alienation:

> It [estranged labor] changes for him the *life of the species* into a means of individual life. First it estranges the life of the species and individual life, and secondly it makes individual life in its abstract form the purpose of the life of the species, likewise in its abstract and estranged form[14].

However, he fails to liberate himself from the tenacious influence of that abstract theoretical subject-object scheme which has entrenched itself in Western Thought. Marx, thus, succumbs to the traditional tendency to approach human community and human freedom in terms of these abstract theoretical categories. This is apparent from the quote given above where Marx speaks of human community as rooted in man's capacity to make the community "his object . . . in practice and in theory", and when he differentiates between man and the animals:

> The animal is immediately one with its life activity. It does not distinguish itself from it. It is *its life activity*. Man makes his life activity itself the object of his will and of his consciousness. He has conscious life activity. It is not a determination with which he directly merges. Conscious life activity distinguishes man immediately from animal life activity. It is just because of this that he is a species being. Or rather, it is only because he is a species being that he is a conscious being, i.e., that his own life is an object for him. Only because of that is his activity free activity[15].

13 *Ibid.*, p. 112.
14 *Ibid.*, p. 112-113.
15 *Ibid.*, p. 113.

Thus, we see that human community is closely related to man's ability to objectify. The word "being" (*Wesen*) used in this passage might better have been translated as "essence". This essence is something that can be grasped in theoretical categories: it becomes clear to one by means of theoretical objectification. In other words, human community only becomes possible if everyone, in a sense, duplicates himself by objectifying himself. For when a person objectifies himself he places himself over against himself. Man-as-object appears over against man-as-subject; of course, there is an identity that somehow persists. In fact, since man-as-subject and man-as-object are so proximate in identity, the latter being, in a sense, the result of the objectifying activity of the former, individualism is not yet wholly precluded.

Because of this close proximity between the self-as-object and the self-as-subject, Marx has not yet given us a sufficient condition for human community. If everyone duplicates himself by objectifying himself, community is possible; thus, objectification is a necessary condition. But the duplicating subject seems to be conceived of as an individual subject: each person has to duplicate himself. Thus, objectification is not a sufficient condition. In order to have his process of duplication through objectification answer to the requirement of community, Marx needs a more universal basis. An aggregate of duplicated individuals does not compose a real community.

2.9.   The more universal basis that Marx resorts to is the object world as world:

> It is just in his work upon the objective world, therefore, that man first really proves himself to be a *species being*. This production is his active species life. Through and because of this production, nature appears as *his* work and his reality. The object of labor is, therefore, the *objectification of man's species life*: for he duplicates himself not only, as in consciousness, intellectually, but also actively, in reality, and therefore he contemplates himself in a world that he has created[16].

As the passage makes clear, the objectivity of that world does not exclude its amenability to human cultivation. But it is its objectivity that provides the universal basis that Marx requires to make objectification more communal. However, even in this passage Marx's approach to community remains determined by the theoretical subject-object scheme. When he says that we observe this process of objectification and duplication occurring not only intellectually, but also actively, i.e., in man's labor, we detect his emphasis on practice: activity as man's primary and authentic mode of self-expression. He maintained this over against the Hegelian apotheosis of abstract contemplation. However, amazingly enough, Marx goes on to say that even this practical

[16] *Ibid.*, p. 114.

process culminates in man's "contemplating" himself in the world "out there" that he has created by his labor, his objectification. Thus, the primacy of the theoretical, of the spectator attitude, that Marx condemned in Hegel, creeps back into Marx's own views. In other words, man becomes a real species-being, a real community when together with his fellowman he can *contemplate* his works which have become embodied over against himself in the objective, communal world.

Although we have not hereby analysed Marx's essay, *"Estranged Labor"*, to the end, the comments that we have made serve adequately as a transition to the next essay that we wish to examine, *"Private Property and Communism"*. In the latter essay he presents communism as the only way of surmounting the self-alienation and self-estrangement which he analysed in the essay we have just looked at. We have followed Marx's analysis of the situation using his terminology, now we will see whether his solution *via* communism is a valid solution, also according to his own standards.

3. *Private Property and Communism*

Marx presents communism as the supersession or transcendence of the self-alienation of labor. But communism does not fall ready-made from heaven; it is a process that develops along a certain course:

> The transcendence of self-estrangement follows the same course as self-estrangement[17].

The rest of the essay deals with the main phases that this course of development passes through. Again, true to the Idealist and Marxist penchant for triads, three such phases are detected. We will deal with each of these in turn.

3.1. The first phase that the supersession of self-estrangement has to undergo is not yet a radical change; in fact, it is even a culmination of evils already inherent in the relationships established by private property.

> By embracing this relation as a *whole*, communism is: In its first form only a *generalization* and *consummation* of this relationship... the dominion of *material* property bulks so large that it wants to destroy *everything* which is not capable of being possessed by all as *private property*... In negating the *personality* of man in every sphere, this type of communism is really nothing but the logical expression of private property, which is its negation. General *envy* constituting itself as a power is the disguise in which *greed* reestablishes itself and satisfies itself, only in *another* way... The crude communism is only the culmination of this envy and of this leveling-down proceeding from the *preconceived* minimum. It has a *definite, limited* standard[18].

17 *Ibid.*, p. 132.
18 *Ibid.*, p. 132-3.

Central to Marx's concern here is the notion of self-estrangement; in other words, a factual, historical state of affairs which he has called self-estrangement functions as a normative model for Marx. This state of affairs directs his argument, his ideas of change and also of improvement. Accordingly, the supersession or transcendence of self-estrangement follows the same course as self-estrangement itself. An almost inexorable law determines the course of both. Thus, Marx's thought is orientated to the world of material objects "over against" man – a world in which material needs and property are dominant. These were, as we also pointed out above, central factors in the situation of self-estrangement.

However, at the same time, Marx wants to replace this situation in which material things are dominant; otherwise there would be no real supersession. The law we referred to does not, therefore, imply an eternal recurrence of the same. Marx believes in progress and melioration. So although the first phase is an inevitable one, he is yet able to call it a "crude" phase because it is the culmination of the greed and envy that constitute private property. It is, according to Marx, the negation of human personality and of the "entire world of culture and civilization". It remains fixed on the world of material objects; indeed, it is the culmination of that fixation. Yet, at the same time, it demonstrates the untenability of this fixation or negation because it generalizes the greed implicit in the world of private property. Thus, is also shows how untenable the negation of the whole world of culture and civilization is. Already in this first phase we can detect a certain striving toward the establishment of a positive community. For the complete generalization of the negation that dominates the world of private property and that occurs in the phase of "crude communism" is at once a transition to a more authentic community of persons, that is, a community no longer exclusively concentrated on and estranged in the world of material objects. It is to this duality that Marx refers when he says:

> The first positive annulment of private property – *crude* communism – is thus merely one *form* in which the vileness of private property, which wants to set itself up as the *positive community*, comes to the surface[19].

Now that the untenability of this individualistic form of society has become obvious through its generalization in that phase of crude communism, the beginning of a real society is made possible in phase two. (Marx is speaking of this individualistic form when he speaks of society dominated by private property; we discussed this above when we explained Hegel's concept of civil society). Within this second phase there are two possibilities:

---

[19] *Ibid.*, p. 134-5.

Communism (a) still political in nature – democratic or despotic; (b) with the abolition of the state, yet still incomplete, and being still affected by private property (i.e., by the estrangement of man)[20].

The first possibility, the politically determined society still implies a certain kind of estrangement for Marx. Although it might provide a certain transcendence of self-estrangement, it might at the same time introduce a new form of self-estrangement. To understand this, we have to recall Hegel's view of the state. To Hegel, the state was the expression of the moral idea. A politically determined society reminded Marx of this Hegelian notion of the state, and as we saw, Marx considered this an idealistic, moralistic, formalistic and abstract notion. It entailed an escape into an ideal sphere. Marx wishes to locate authentic human community in society, not in the state. Society for Marx is not politically determined but it is that organism with needs to be satisfied. At the same time, these needs had to be humanized; for "A radical revolution has ultimately to be a revolution of radical needs". This is what Marx is referring to when he says:

> ... but since it has not yet grasped the positive essence of private property, and just as little the *human* nature of need, it remains captive to it and infected by it[21].

A full-fledged communism has to be aware of the human nature of its needs and to humanize them. Both forms of this second phase are still affected by private property, but there is some degree of progress over the first phase; man is turned away from his absorption and lostness in the world of material objects:

> In both forms communism already is aware of being reintegration or return of man to himself, the transcendence of human self-estrangement; ... [22].

The final phase presupposes the two earlier phases and profits from them:

> ... *Communism* as the *positive* transcendence of *private property*, as *human self-estrangement*, and therefore as the real *appropriation of the human* essence by and for man; communism therefore as the complete return of man to himself as a *social* (i.e., human) being – a return become conscious, and accomplished within the entire wealth of previous development[23].

This phase does not exist yet, but Marx announces its advent in glowing words:

> Communism as the *positive* transcendence of *private property*, as [of] *human self-estrangement*, ... is the *genuine* resolution of the conflict between man and

20 *Ibid.*, p. 135.
21 *Ibid.*, p. 135.
22 *Ibid.*, p. 135.
23 *Ibid.*, p. 135.

nature and between man and man... Communism is the riddle of history solved, and it knows itself to be this solution[24].

3.2. It appears that Marx has *presupposed* an antagonism or conflict between man and nature and between man and man, not merely as a factual situation, but also as a condition for the success of both his theory regarding historical development and his perspective supplied by the theory. In order to clarify what we mean by this statement, we first ask the question: Is the resolution that Marx offers genuine according to the standards supplied by the framework of his own thought? Already at the outset when he began by positing a parallel development between the supersession of self-estrangement and self-estrangement itself, he created little chance for a *real* resolution or *breakthrough* of the situation. The source of the problem is rooted in Marx's theory of the *succession* of the three phases. It is the problem of the *"Umschlag"* (the "turn-over" or transition). Marx distinguishes different phases, but if he wants to maintain that these are different phases in a single development, then he should describe the *how* of the succession, transition and continuity. There is a mystery or riddle here that has not been solved by Marx. His construction of different phases would have been much more convincing if, from the beginning, he would have assumed the existence of some force or dynamic factor pervading, first of all, the historical process of self-estrangement, and second, the supersession of that self-estrangement. Then he would have had some basis for his idea of succession and of progress, and for the continuity of the whole process. Now he has to appeal to a mysterious notion of *"Umschlag"*. To simply state that at a certain point a new phase starts by way of an *"Umschlag"*, a "turn-over", is inadequate. The assumption of a pervasive dynamic which governs the whole process would have provided a means of relativizing self-estrangement. This self-estrangement could then have been considered as a contingent stage that occurred in history, with or without some "rationality" of its own. It could then be regarded as something, also, that had entered into the continuous dynamic of history but which could, therefore, not be regarded as a necessary condition for this dynamic. Only on such a basis could Marx have made sense of both the continuity of the process as well as the supersession of self-estrangement. Because he does not provide a clear and adequate concept of continuity, of a dynamic factor that pervades the whole process of history, Marx's concept of self-estrangement plays, of necessity, an ambiguous role in his tought.

3.3. Self-estrangement is, on the one hand, a necessary ingredient of human existence for Marx. This is due to his historicism. Historicism

[24] *Ibid.*, p. 135.

80

postulates that human existence is only given to us in its historical horizon. Since the historical situation is ultimate, the analysis of human existence can only deal with man as he has become in the present historical societal situation. Because of this historicism, self-estrangement becomes a necessary and essential element in human history, not merely an accidental and contingent element. Self-estrangement is indispensable to human development and progress (albeit negatively).

However, the very term self-estrangement, on the other hand, implies criticism. The historical situation as such, which we have to take as the starting point for our analysis of human existence, can no longer be simply accepted as is. There is a value judgement implicit in the term self-estrangement: it points out that history is infected by inhumanity. This self-estrangement must be overcome by establishing a situation of genuinely human communism. However, were this latter situation achieved, then history in the first sense, in which self-estrangement played an indispensable role, would be abolished. Marx tries to solve this problem by calling development prior to the establishment of a genuine human communism only *pre-history*. Then the situation in which self-estrangement has been overcome is the beginning of genuine history. Obviously, he has only hereby achieved a verbal solution.

3.4.   Marx claims a lot for this final phase of communism; he culminates his pretentious claims and expectations with the statement that "Communism is the riddle of history solved, and it *knows itself to be this solution* [italics added]". Earlier Marx's idea of the supersession of human self-estrangement in labor culminated in the laborer contemplating his own product. This statement expresses a similar idea. Again it is knowledge, by which Marx means theoretical knowledge, that is the consummation of the whole historical process. Thus, Marx's debt to Hegel surfaces once again; for Hegel, also, the final consummation of history was the self-consciousness of a knowing mind. The difference from Hegel is that Marx builds his construction on the material basis of needs.

3.5.   Although it may seem so, this is not really Marx's final word on the ultimate goal of history. When Marx speaks of the "*genuine* resolution of the conflict between man and nature and between man and man", it would seem that for Marx this phase of communism is the ultimate reconciliation of all conflicts in history. At this point there is no intimation of anything beyond; for is this stage not the genuine integration of man and the establishment of authentic human community? However, when we turn to the end of the manuscript, we detect a certain dissatisfaction on the part of Marx with regard to this final human solution as the ultimate goal of history.

This section is rather difficult to translate, especially because certain words in the manuscript were almost wholly obscured so that they had to be filled in with likely conjectures. Therefore, we quote two different renderings:

> Communism is the position as the negation of the negation, and is hence the *actual* phase necessary for the next stage of historical development in the process of human emancipation and rehabilitation. *Communism* is the necessary pattern and the dynamic principle of the immediate future, but communism as such is not the goal of human development – which goal is the structure of human society[25].

> Communism is the phase of negation of the negation and is, consequently, for the next stage of historical development, a real and necessary factor in the emancipation and rehabilitation of man. Communism is the necessary form and the dynamic principle of the immediate future, but communism is not itself the goal of human development – the form of human society[26].

In a note to this passage, Struik mentions:

> Since the manuscript ends here, we can only guess what the meaning of this last sentence is. Milligan believes that by "communism as such" is meant crude, egalitarian, communism, such as that propounded by Babeuf and his followers. However, since Marx speaks of communism as the necessary shape of the next future, as the "negation of negation", he may well have thought of human emancipation beyond the abolition of private property, to a "synthesis" in an even richer stage of human emancipation, after alienation has been conquered. He returns to this point in the next section ["The Meaning of Human Requirements"], but here again the text has been mutilated[27].

Apparently, Marx is saying that the ultimate goal of history cannot be identified with one of the stages of its development. Although communism is the final stage, it is a stage, nevertheless; as such, it is related to the previous stages and even presupposes them. Thus, it also presupposes the conflicts or negativity that characterizes these stages. While it comprises a new position, it remains a negation of a negation, and as such it must be considered a relative or intermediary position. Thus, communism cannot be regarded as being the ultimate goal, for that goal must be absolute and fully positive, unadulterated by any echos of negativity.

This does not appear to be placing an unwarranted construction on Marx's words, for if we make use of the triadic scheme so dear to Marx himself, we end up with a similar interpretation. Within that scheme, communism appeared as the final supersession or reconciliation of the opposition between the prior affirmation and the prior negation. Although it appeared as the negation of the negation, it remains one of the components of the dialectical scheme; it has overcome negativity, yet it still includes it.

[25] *Ibid.*, p. 146.
[26] T. B. Bottomore, *Karl Marx Early Writings*, p. 167.
[27] *Ibid.*, p. 245.

3.6.   Uncertain as the interpretation of these sentences may be, it seems clear that Marx is struggling with the relativity and artificiality of his whole dialectical scheme. The obscurity of these sentences could also be a reflection of Marx's own inability to break through the problems posed by the dialectical scheme of his thought. He further seems to imply that the ultimate goal cannot be stated in terms of the dialectical scheme of which communism is the final component. There is a hint that Marx considers this ultimate goal to be a factor that *governs* or *directs* the whole process of development without itself being part of that development. This, then, may be an attempt at supplying that dynamic factor which we pointed out earlier was lacking in his theory. What exactly that goal entails is difficult to say. In his later works such observations become very rare. When they do appear, they tend towards utopianism.

He does at times speak of a realm of freedom as opposed to the realm of necessity, for example, in *Das Kapital*. But we can only live and think in the realm of necessity. The realm of freedom is not really conceivable by the intellectual means available to us. For our dialectical understanding is suited to the things and events of the realm of necessity. That understanding enables us to predict certain processes and developments which are based upon a certain dialectical necessity in the course of events. The realm of freedom is beyond this realm and is not amenable to conceptualization. But although we cannot conceptualize that realm, we nevertheless have to postulate it in order to provide ultimate direction to the developments within the realm of necessity.

3.7.   We are here touching on the very roots of Marx's thought and of problems inherent in his thought. This is part of the reason for the density of the sentences we have considered and for their vacillation and ambiguity. Their scarcity in his later works, we may surmise, results from a channeling of Marx's concern into two main directions. First, he wanted his economic and philosophical works to function as eye-openers to contemporary society. He wanted to combat the inclination to conceal the real facts and inner tendency of the development of his society. He saw himself as a dis-coverer, in the literal sense of the word. In the second place, he wanted to concentrate the attention of society on the class struggle that he dis-covered as one of the "facts" of contemporary society, and then develop a strategy and practical tactics for that struggle. This practical role gives us Marx the agitator. Because of this dual concern, Marx's idea of an ultimate goal remained undeveloped. But in the final passage of this essay, Marx provides some hints regarding the nature of this ultimate goal. We quote the entire last paragraph:

> But since for the socialist man the *entire so-called history of the world* is nothing but the creation of man through human labor, nothing but the emergence

of nature for man, so he has the visible, irrefutable proof of his *birth* through himself, of the *process of his creation*. Since the *real existence* of man and nature – since man has become for man as the being of nature, and nature for man as the being of man has become practical, sensuous, perceptible – the question about an *alien* being, about a being above nature and man – a question which implies the admission of the unreality of nature and of man – has become impossible in practice. *Atheism*, as the denial of this unreality, has no longer any meaning, for atheism is a *negation of God*, and postulates the *existence of man* through this negation; but socialism as socialism no longer stands in any need of such a mediation. It proceeds from the *practically and theoretically sensuous consciousness* of man and of nature as the *essence*. Socialism is man's *positive self-consciousness*, no longer mediated through the annulment of religion, just as *real life* is man's positive reality, no longer mediated through the annulment of private property, through *communism*. Communism is the position as the negation of the negation, and is hence the *actual* phase necessary for the next stage of historical development in the process of human emancipation and rehabilitation. *Communism* is the necessary pattern and the dynamic principle of the immediate future, but communism as such is not the goal of human development – which goal is the structure of human society[28].

Marx uses the term "socialism". That ultimate fully positive situation will manifest a form in which man is first a truly social being. In this socialist situation two facets may be distinguished: the facet of human consciousness and the facet of reality.

In distinguishing that first facet, Marx says that socialism is man's positive self-consciousness, no longer mediated through the negation of religion. Furthermore, it is a true unity, for it comprises man's consciousness of his roots in nature. He expresses this same notion in the first sentence quoted: " ... the *entire so-called history of the world* is nothing but the creation of man through human labor, nothing but the emergence of nature for man, so he has the visible, irrefutable proof of his *birth* through himself, of the *process of his creation*". In other words, man's self-production through his own labor is at the same time a process of natural birth. By the way, Marx here also clearly betrays how much his thought is still in continuity with the basic idea of the "Renaissance" (literally: re-birth).

Because of the close relationship that this positive self-consciousness has to nature, its essential form is that of a sensuous consciousness: " ... socialism as socialism no longer stands in any need of such a mediation. It proceeds from the *practically and theoretically sensuous consciousness* of man and of nature as the essence." This sensuous consciousness refers to Marx's notion that felt needs and the urge to satisfy those needs are basic to man's consciousness of self. This notion, thus, contains a hidden polemic against the traditional idea of self-consciousness as a sophisticated, intellectual and highly abstract consciousness. For confirmation we briefly refer to Marx's essay, *Critique*

[28] *Ibid.*, p. 145-6.

of Hegel's Dialectic and General Philosophy, where he once again evokes Feuerbach's support. In setting forth Feuerbach's contribution to critical theory, he lists for his third achievement:

> ... to have opposed to the negation of the negation which claims to be the absolute positive, a self-subsistent principle positively founded on itself.
> Feuerbach explains Hegel's dialectic, and at the same time justifies taking the positive phenomenon, that which is perceptible and indubitable, as the starting-point ... [29].

What we wanted to notice in this passage is Marx's appreciation for Feuerbach's assertion of the sensuous consciousness in opposition to Hegel's sophisticated, abstract theoretical mind.

In the light of this position, it is curious that Marx continues to speak of a "practically *and theoretically* sensuous consciousness". One would be inclined to think that sensuous consciousness could not be theoretical at all. Perhaps Marx is here only making room for his own theoretical enterprise. Marx, then, seems to view his theoretical enterprise as a demonstration and confirmation of what man was already conscious of in a more practical way, at a more basic, immediate level of feeling. However, for our purpose it is sufficient to point out how this positive self-consciousness serves to characterize socialism.

The other facet of socialism that Marx refers to is the reality which that consciousness is a consciousness of. He calls it "real life": "Socialism is man's *positive self-consciousness*, no longer mediated through the annulment of religion, just as *real life* is man's positive reality, no longer mediated through the annulment of private property, through *communism*". This real life or positive reality is related to man's self-creation through his labor which is at the same time the emergence of nature for man. In his labor, in the manufacturing of products man is brought so close to nature, to reality in its visible and tangible immediacy, that this can serve as a "visible, irrefutable proof of his *birth* through himself".

We can extrapolate from the hints dropped by Marx in this passage and get some notion of the kind of ultimate goal or situation that he envisions. His socialism is that of a direct, immediate life of all men together. Together they experience an immediate sensuous relationship to nature. This sensuous relationship is achieved not through passivity, but through activity, namely, productive labor. With his advocacy of "immediacy" Marx is repudiating the artificial intermediaries of (too) abstract concepts, of (too) mechanical tools and apparatus, and of (too) indirect symbols. We insert the "too" because Marx wavers between wanting to eliminate, e.g., abstract concepts altogether and between wanting only to temper their abstractness in the realization that they

[29] T. B. Bottomore, *Karl Marx Early Writings*, p. 197-8.

just cannot be totally eliminated. All these artificial intermediaries detract from real, positive life and from the sensuous consciousness corresponding to it.

In this vision that Marx has conceived of the kingdom of mankind we can detect the operation of the two ideals we pointed out earlier. First, there is the humanistic ideal of human freedom with man revolving about himself as his own true sun. Applied to labor it meant that man in labor creates himself. In the second place, there is the ideal that man's life and society could be comprehensively, theoretically and scientifically accounted for, both as they are and as they develop. Because this scientific explanation of the laws governing the development of life has to account for that life in its entirety, including its negativity, conflicts and suffering, the dialectical method was introduced. These two ideals are obviously antagonistic. Marx's final "idyl" – his vision of man's ultimate form of community – should be understood against the background of the tension between these two ideals.

CHAPTER VI

Some key notions of Marx

1. *Marx's New Conception of Philosophy*

In order to understand Marx's enterprise as a whole and the reason for its influence, it is necessary to notice that he is developing a new conception of philosophy. We have already referred to Marcuse's continuation of this theme. Marcuse distinguishes between philosophy in the traditional sense and a critical theory of society. The term society used here includes the sciences. Marcuse wants to unmask the involvement of the so-called empirical sciences in this society. He reveals the empirical character of these sciences to be largely pseudo-empirical; for they include little or no awareness of how their basic concepts and their general framework are predetermined by the current ideas of this society. Scientists-duped, unsuspecting victims unaware – promote the establishment in their empirical work. The philosophies whose basic tenets are oriented to these sciences, especially neo-positivism and analytic philosophy, are even worse in this respect than these sciences themselves[1]. Although Marcuse cannot be said to set forth an altogether orthodox Marxism, he is right in emphasizing Marx's awareness of himself as standing at a critical and crucial point in the historical development of philosophy. Marx felt that although philosophy had been striving to be critical for a long time, its method of criticism had been too general, too abstract, and far too aloof from the real issues of society. Philosophy had to become more directly relevant to these issues. It is this same awareness that Marcuse picks up in his distinction between philosophy in the traditional sense and as a critical theory of society[2].

Marx rightly felt that the relationship of philosophy to the fullness of experience had become obscured. The fullness of our experience is first of all non-scientific and continues to be so even after the appearance of science. *Non*-scientific is not to be confused with unscientific; the latter would mean in contradiction to the standards of science;

---

[1] *Cf.* Chapter 8 & 9 of *One-Dimensional Man.*
[2] Marx overestimated the newness of this idea, for Plato was already well aware of the critical function of philosophy over toward society.

whereas, non-scientific intends to point to the fact that experience is much broader than just scientific knowledge. Marx saw that philosophy had become more and more irrelevant to life's concreteness and fullness. This insight was heightened all the more through his acquaintance with the philosophy of Hegel, which claimed to be critical and, at the same time, all-encompassing. Marx reasoned that if Hegel's philosophy is the logical outcome of traditional philosophy and if it presumes to be the final, comprehensive word about man, his world and his society, then the time had come for a new interpretation of the task of philosophy. The inadequacy, abstractness and irrelevancy of Hegel's philosophy to life was felt all too keenly by Marx.

2. Marx's Notion of "Critical"

The society that Marx lived in was torn apart by and suffered under traumatic changes not only of the Industrial Revolution but also of the French Revolution and the resulting conservative reactions. The grand system of Hegel was supposed to encompass even the miseries and sufferings of contemporary family and factory life in its negations. In Hegel's philosophical showroom, negativity or evil is located among the essential truths or undeniable states of affairs that philosophy objectively describes or interprets. Marx saw this as an estrangement of philosophy from its proper critical function. For the historical role of philosophy is the intensification of man's critical self-consciousness. Thus, philosophy unmasks religion as just such an attempt to escape from self-consciousness. However, when negativity, conflict, suffering, evil gets its own ascribed niche in the objective showroom of philosophy so that it becomes something to be contemplated, then philosophy serves to affirm the *status quo*. As such, it becomes another form of estrangement, like religion, for it does everything but intensify man's critical self-consciousness.

Genuinely critical thought is directly relevant to our human existence and to our being human (human being); it is thought directed towards the service of humanity; it is a "demonstration *ad hominem*". An often quoted statement of Marx – one of his "Theses on Feuerbach" – is: "Philosophers have only interpreted the world in different ways; the point is to change it". Philosophy itself becomes involved in the practical struggle for the change, in fact, the revolution of society. It becomes a *means* in this struggle. The question that remains is: does it function as an expedient or as a *mean of power*?

3. Marx's Notion of "Historical"

Another concept that we encounter frequently in Marx's writings is the notion of the "historical". Actually the notion already recurred very often in Hegel's writings. To both Hegel and Marx it indicates that man and his society are not fixed: man *produces himself*. This process is called history. For Marx this process of self-production is further characterized by dynamic *needs* and drives or *forces*. Especially in his later works, Marx further qualifies these needs and drives as economically determined. The development of these needs and drives or forces evidence a certain continuity. For example, it is possible to trace the development from feudal society to civil or bourgeois society. However, there are always antagonistic forces present that oppose development. Here the necessity for or the call to revolution enters in. The existing conditions of production can no longer accommodate the new drives or forces of production which history has created. This situation forces a choice between either suppressing these new drives or forces, or employing them to break through the existing conditions. The former reactionary alternative is, of course, not a viable one for Marx: stopping these new drives or forces is impossible.

When the term "historical" becomes prefixed to "philosophy", we can detect a connection with our earlier concept of "critical". When Marx says that it is important to philosophize historically, he means that it is the duty of philosophy to recognize and point out critical historical situations and reveal their ripeness for revolution. In this unmasking, philosophy itself becomes a historical power, for it contradicts (i.e., speaks against) the existing situation in its positive, established character. By deliberately compromising that situation, philosophy opens possibilities for change.

Inevitably Marx must face the question whether his view of society and historical development is just a description of bare facts or whether it is itself an *interpretation*. In the light of this question we ask: what happens to the earlier contrast we saw Marx set up between an abstract, detached, intellectual philosophy and one that is engaged and critical, a protest? What does Marx mean when he calls for philosophy to stop appealing to or presenting universal interpretations of established or given states of affairs? Does not such a philosophy, that foregoes an appeal to some state of affairs, become purely eschatological, that is, a prophecy and advertisement for a preconceived future? Then, in its theoretical aspect such a philosophy becomes utopian, while in its practical aspect it becomes an incitement to violence. Utopia and violence are usually siblings[3].

[3] This is, for example, what Karl Popper repeatedly criticizes in the totalitarian conception of Marxism (and in other totalitarian conceptions as well). For him, however, there exists no reasonable *integral* approach to mankind and society, or to the diagnosis of its diseases. His alternative is: *either* totalitarian (with its adverse consequences) *or* "social engineering", which attempts to improve conditions by "trial and error" and "piecemeal".

But Marx does appeal to historical reality. That historical reality gives obvious evidence of human self-estrangement; in fact, that self-estrangement is total; it affects man as a species being. Both capitalist and proletariat share in it. But it is especially in the proletariat that the absolute and radical suffering that comprises the negativity of history embodies itself. The radical character of this suffering forms a limiting situation in its dehumanization of human existence so that a genuine possibility for radical self-recognition and self-redemption arises. This suffering involves a rediscovery by the proletariat of the fundamental trait of human existence, for it refers not to a merely external state of affairs, but to a state of affairs that is experienced immediately, radically and concretely. This fundamental human trait Marx calls *Leidenschaft*, which may, like the Latin *passio*, be translated as either passion or suffering. In this rediscovery man finds himself to be a being with real needs, a being who wants something other outside of himself and also other people. Nevertheless, he finds these needs within himself, so that his striving to satisfy these needs is really a striving for self-realization. Therefore, Marx can speak of self-redemption even while pointing to our need for the other. It is only when a universal class of men, the proletariat, appeared on the historical scene - a class that experienced this suffering, this dehumanization, this negativity – only then could the philosophy of Marxism appear. Thus, Marx wants to make his philosophy credible by appealing to this given: concrete human suffering. He does not wish merely to be a prophet or to spin out utopias.

In our discussion of the first essay, we discovered insurmountable tensions and polarities in Marx's views on the position and the role of philosophy with respect to both the existence of the proletariat and their struggle for practical emancipation. In this connection, we discussed the "arm of criticism" and the "criticism of arms". These tensions and discords persist throughout Marx's writings; they are basic, ultimate elements in his thought which he could not overcome. As a result, he is unable to provide a truly radical and integral view for the redemption of man in his society.

Although our critique of Marx issues from a Christian commitment, we cannot, in contradiction to the Marxists, pretend that we, on the other hand, do *possess* such a view. Or that we, in contradistinction to the Marxists, are capable of redeeming and reforming man in his society. We must confess that we are no longer able to establish out of ourselves the *nature of the given, not* by means of an autonomous philosophy *nor* by means of the experience of suffering. We must learn to accept the given as it is revealed to us and then it can direct our philosophy and even our suffering accordingly. Mankind, society and history are in even worse straits than Marx felt them to be. The suffering and cross of Christ tell us how much worse. Moreover, all our desperate attempts at self-recognition and self-redemption are deceptions and illusions. Even a small community like a family, which is based more on a bond of moral love rather than a power relationship, cannot maintain itself on the basis of these notions of self-recognition and self-redemption. Self-denial is the reverse side of radical belief in and radical surrender to Jesus Christ. That self-denial involves the radical denial of our own power of self-recognition and self-redemption and also of our own ability to establish what is given, whether through thought or suffering. By such self-surrender we become part of the power, the grace and the redemption of Jesus Christ; for he desires to include us in a new mankind, with a new hope. Out of this surrender a new *activity* arises which cannot be circumscribed by any of our current descriptions of "activity".

4. Marx's Notion of "Dialectic"

The concept of dialectical has to be understood in close relation to the concept of historical. We have seen that history, according to Marx and Hegel, is the process of man's self-production. Man and his society are not fixed but developing entities; they are in a process of becoming, in a process of self-production that proceeds in and *via* polar opposi-tions. It is essential to this process that a certain position or a realized, established state of affairs does not merely continue in a pure identity with itself, but that it provoke a negation. This negation reveals the limitations of the first position, of the first established state of affairs. In this way, new possibilities are also revealed which are open to realization. However, this position and its negation, taken in themselves, stand over against each other and continue in a polar tension over toward each other. This tension demonstrates their need for each other in the sense that the first position itself provokes its own negation, but that negation is still a negation of that position. Thus, the two refer to each other. However, at the same time, they repel each other. As long as the polarity continues there is the possibility of something new, but not yet the realization of the new. The possibility of something new is evidenced by the appearance of the negation, but since it is only a negation, it is not yet a new reality. This new reality first appears in the synthesis, which is the formation of a more comprehensive whole that incorporates both the original position and the negation as limited parts of the greater whole. Marx also calls this incorporation "appropri-ation". The earlier polar tension called for this solution or synthesis; but in due time this new synthesis will reveal its unique limitations and the process will begin all over again. This synthesis, thus, becomes

91

another positive starting point that evokes a new negation and then a new and even more comprehensive synthesis.

The terms "position" and "negation" give the impression of being neutral logical terms that can be applied objectively without relying on value judgements. However, they usually carry definite connotations of such judgements. As the original or established position, capitalist society is called positive, but in another sense it is also called negative; whereas, the proletariat and the revolution is the destructive negation of capitalist society, yet it is also called positive. There is another level of ambiguity contained in the term "negation" or "negativity". It refers not only to the conflicts and competition involved in achieving certain unattained goals, but also includes in the power struggle the brokenness and disharmony that the Christian recognizes as the fruit of sin. Thus, their usage is constantly ambiguous. Marx seems to wish to maintain the impression that he is just using a neutral instrument to supply an objective interpretation of history, but at the same time the terms exhibit a definite evaluative viewpoint.

The tension or polar opposition that Marx posits between the original position and its negation is conceived of as arising out of given conditions of production and the forces of production. The conditions of production and the forces of production need each other; but at the same time they are continually at odds. This tension is necessary for the progress of the historical process, otherwise it would stagnate. Without the presence of this tension history would resemble Nietzsche's eternal recurrence of the same. Thus, dialectic, in attempting to combine logic and history, caused confusion and distortion in both areas. The struggle for power in history had to be explained in such traditional logical terms as thesis, negation, affirmation and the principle of contradiction. This yielded a rigid and meager explanation of history. Logic, on the other hand, had to be reinterpreted so that it could account for the appearance of something new in history[4].

However, a dialectic exists in Marx's thought that is more basic and deeper than this polarity between the conditions and the forces of production. This basic dialectic is that between man himself as he exists in his own individual sphere and that which is external to man, including other men. To put it differently, a dialectic exists between the needs and possibilities possessed (really "owned") by the self *and*

---

[4] This is not to say that any attempt to relate "history" and "logic" (or rather the historical and the logical "aspect" of reality) is as such senseless or mistaken. To say that "history" is not "rational" does not imply that it is essentially "irrational" and thoroughly unanalysable. Conversely, to say that logic is a "system" with elements and rules of its own, does not prevent us from conceiving of this "system" as an *open* one, open also to elements and normativities of a specifically historical nature. The author cannot here elaborate these statements.

those things and persons necessary for the realization of those needs and possibilities. We discussed this bifurcation of man according to a subject-object scheme in connection with Marx's definition of man as a species-being. The idea of self-alienation is largely determined by this basic dialectic. Because everyone is so structured that his positive awareness of his needs and possibilities reveals his need of something and someone outside of himself, self-alienation is not just a chance occurrence in history or something alien that can be eliminated, but an indispensible element in the progressive development of history, i.e., in the process of man's self-production in society.

In this notion of self-alienation we once again encounter the ambivalence that we pointed out in his use of the terms "positive" and "negative". As an indispensable element of history self-alienation cannot be gotten rid of. Yet, it is also something that ought not to be, something antinormative, which should ultimately be overcome in the goal of a completely human and positive socialism. Marx tries to eliminate or tone down this ambivalence in several ways.

First, he projects the ultimate goal, or as he calls it in *Das Kapital* the realm of freedom, into a transcendent sphere, a utopian "beyond" that functions as a beckoning ideal. But then it can no longer serve as a real directive principle for his philosophical thought.

Another way that Marx tries to remove the ambivalence in the dialectical tension is his shifting the center of gravity from man to his natural world. He emphasizes the role of the material substructure in historical development; material conditions such as the availability of natural means and resources become primary. However, Marx never attempts to give the natural world an independent status, i.e., a role separate from man and his labor. It involves no more than a shift in emphasis.

Third, he places more and more emphasis on the class struggle and on the urgent demands for practical involvement in that struggle. In this connection, philosophy is seen more as a practical instrument; it gets a more pragmatic function in conceiving strategy for and agitating in favor of the class struggle.

5. Marx's Notion of "Materialistic"

This category was referred to above under Marx's second method for toning down the ambivalence in the concept of self-alienation, namely, by emphasizing the material substructure. We also encountered this same element much earlier when Marx stated that revolution needed a passive element or a material basis. As we pointed out, this element plays an ever increasing role in the development of his thought. He qualifies it economically in terms of conditions of production. These conditions of production, in turn, are dependent upon available natural energy sources. The technical exploitation and control of these resources is of cardinal importance to the development of society. Despite his opposition to it as an establishment philosophy, Marx shares this emphasis with positivism.

Included in this material basis are man's needs, i.e., immediately experienced needs such as hunger, thirst, shelter, etc. Also included are the means immediately available to satisfy those needs, the first of which is the bodily apparatus of the laborer. In this connection Marx especially stresses the function of hand labor; true *manu*-facturing, as the Latin root implies, is done by hand.

A tension exists within the material substructure: between the given conditions of production on the one hand and the experienced needs and means for satisfying those needs on the other hand. The real motivating force for the forward movement of society resides, not in the given conditions of production, but in the acute experience of needs (suffering) and in the bodily force and drive of the laborer to satisfy these needs. In the first essay that we dealt with, Marx stated that material force can only be overthrown by material force. Thus, the motivating power of society appears as a destructive power over against the established conditions of production; for the latter are characterized by the private ownership of both the material resources and the immediate means for satisfying needs. Even the bodily force and drive of the laborer is owned by the capitalist. Private ownership of these resources and means has made itself so at home in the established conditions of production that a complicated superstructure has come to be built upon it which, at the same time, serves to justify this economic situation. Thus, this superstructure serves to veil or camouflage the material economic establishment that produced it. Included in this superstructure or second floor are the established systems of right and law, but also politics and traditional morals and philosophy. The establishment deceptively tries to concentrate the attention of culture on the latter level in order to misleadingly divert attention away from the importance of the first floor, the floor of private property.

However, according to Marx, the floor of private property and possession of bodily forces already involves alienation or estrangement from man's direct relationship to nature. Nature or matter is, to use a metaphor, the soil from which we all must live; everything that we manufacture with our practical labor is drawn from there. Therefore, if nature becomes private property, i.e., if its possession is limited to a certain group, then man as a whole no longer retains a direct relationship to nature: in other words, he is, to a certain extent, estranged from it. The establishment of the ideological superstructure means an even further estrangement from that fundamental relationship to nature;

94

in the first place, because it camouflages that estrangement; and secondly, because it provides a new means for the dominant class to oppress the suffering labor class, the proletariat. Although the acute experience of needs and the bodily drive of the laborer to satisfy these needs may appear as a destructive or negative force when it evidences itself as the total revolution of society, it, nevertheless, has its roots in a positive experience, namely, the experience of that direct relationship with nature. The ultimate aim of the total revolution of society is also supposed to be positive: a society without property, without oppression, without class struggle, a society without those camouflaging superstructures, a society with a real, direct, common, socialist life. Thus, the ultimate goal is a restoration or recovery of that positive relationship to nature. However, as we have pointed out before, this is not developed beyond scattered hints in Marx's writings.

Using these hints, let us try to compose a picture of what this societal development of mankind might be. In his later development, Marx emphasizes more and more the material basis for the development of society; thus, although some of this is present already in his early writings, most of it is drawn from his later writings. In the material basis a tension exists between the forces of production and the conditions of production. This tension results in the formation of social groups or classes which stand opposed to each other. Thus, the proletariat "class"[5] stands over against the capitalist class: as the oppressed over against the oppressor. This results, according to Marx, in the class struggle, which in turn generates total revolution, on the one hand, and the building of superstructures and forms of private property, on the other. The ultimate aim of the class struggle and total revolution is to overthrow the oppressive side of the tension. We can picture the process as follows[6] (*see next page*).

This diagram does not mean to suggest that Marx wishes to advocate a full-fledged materialism; even in his later development, when he emphasizes the material basis more and more, he never slips into a rigid deterministic or mechanical materialism. Marx stresses that his is a *historical* or *dialectical* materialism. To him, matter is never pure matter, by which he means to say that the availability and structure of matter never completely determine human existence. Marx's emphasis on the material basis is ultimately made to serve his summons directed to man to

[5] *Class* is here put in quotation marks because, as we pointed out in connection with the first essay, the proletariat is not really, in Marx's opinion, just another group alongside others. The capitalists, however, are a class in the usual sense of the word. Rather, the proletariat is the real, universal class, for it is the harbinger of the new mankind; whereas, the capitalist class is a dying class.
[6] The scheme is taken from R. Heiss, *Die grossen Dialektiker des 19. Jahrhunderts*, Berlin 1963, p. 398.

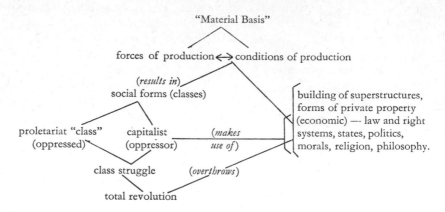

intervene *practically*, to revolt. Such an appeal to man as an active, responsible being would not make sense under a full-fledged materialism.

As long as the dialectic of self-alienation is located primarily in man himself, in the human subject, there is little or no basis for Marx's appeal. For then the alienation is radical: that's just the way man is as a human being. One must then resign himself to the situation. Or at best, one might long for a utopia in which man's inborn alienation has been overcome. But such a utopia could never be accounted for; it remains a mere fiction. However, matter can be manipulated; it is pliable to human purposes; man can change matter and use it to bring about changes. This is why Marx shifts his emphasis to the material basis. Marx's dialectical materialism makes materialism a function of his appeal to man's activity. In thus making this shift in emphasis, however, the place and significance of Marx's own philosophical theory becomes more precarious. Granting for the sake of argument that philosophical theory could be traced back to a material basis, the problem arises when we try to do so with Marx's own theory. Even though it claims to be an ultimate, "revealing" interpretation of the material basis and the tension there extant between the forces and the conditions of production, Marx's philosophy cannot be traced back to that material basis. As we have seen, Marx's attempt to solve this difficulty by pointing to material evidence for the claims of his philosophy in the undeniable existence of the proletariate also falls short. The important thing to notice here, however, is that as Marx becomes more of a materialist in his thinking, his philosophical theory becomes more and more a pragmatic instrument; in fact, it begins to sound like a battle cry.

6. *Final Remarks*

Our discussion of Marx's philosophy has been rather sketchy throughout. However, so is Marx's philosophy itself. But this is no reason to neglect or ignore it. Nor is it a reason to concentrate only on his specifically economic theories. Often his philosophy is so sketchy that interpreting it becomes a difficult and unsatisfying task. Frequently, we would wish for a more elaborate explanation of some of his main concepts and statements. Frequently, too, his arguments are poor. But for all its sketchiness and its inherent problems, his philosophy is undeniably the background to his economic and social theory. The importance of these early manuscripts is that they are the basis and source of his economic and social theory.

Moreover, for all its sketchiness, it is a radical philosophy. It tries to account for its ultimate commitment. And it also tries to express philosophically concerns which are highly relevant to the concreteness and fullness of life. In other words, it attempted to be an universal, integral approach, instead of just a specialistic analysis of certain aspects of life. It is this radicalism which is so instructive and challenging; it challenges us to a serious confrontation, especially in our day.

We have confronted Marx by examining first of all, the [conservative] nature of his expectations with regard to philosophical theory and the precariousness of these expectations. And, then we have shown how, in becoming aware of the precariousness of his expectations, Marx turns into an agitator for the practical, violent overthrow of the existing order; in short, how Marx became the prophet of world revolution.

EPILOGUE

From the Preface and throughout it has become sufficiently clear, I trust, that this book is meant to present a critical analysis down to the very roots of Marx' philosophical thought. Especially, it is meant to offer a critical analysis of the idea and practice of "critique" itself. Is this enough? Should we propose an alternative theory? Earlier I said that this seems impossible on account of what the word "theory" really means. The critical analysis showed, among other things, that theories, even "views" – including possible christian ones – fall short once the real roots are at stake. This is not to say that on more specific and undoubtedly important points an (alternative) view or theory could not be worked out. Outlining and developing such a theory responsibly, however, would require a great deal more than this volume. I think that I have left no doubt concerning at least my *basically* different stance on "man and reality".

Still, some christian readers may feel a certain need to hear just a little more about the guidelines and perspectives that the author would keep in mind when reflecting on some of the issues involved. Non-christian readers would not be unjustified in demanding it. Hence I would close with a number of concluding remarks.

1. *"Religion"*

In placing this notion first one hardly moves away from Marx. "Critique of religion as presupposition of all critique". Well then, I would begin with this: the word "religion" has become so loaded that it is almost useless, both in its Anglo-Saxon and its German contexts; useless, that is, for that which is really at stake.

"The kingdom of God does not consist of words, but in Spirit and Power". The word "spirit" has been subject to much sleight-of-hand also, usually through being opposed to "nature", and as "inner" over against "outer". But "spirit" is like the air in which man lives; it is the breath that we inhale and exhale. It is as "natural" as can be, and a circuit of in-and-out that does not lend itself to a polarization of internal-external. It is the power-source providing man with fuel for all his activities, including his shaping of language. "Religion" is: surrender and power at once.

Marx has not managed to settle accounts with this reality. It is there in his own life and thought, sometimes explicit (cf. pp. 34 ff.), sometimes as a hidden motivation. This is certainly no reason for reproach or criticism. What can and should be criticized is the fact that Marx has not really made clear the relation of his philosophy to this reality, and has instead "suppressed" it – even when his intense awareness of human self-estrangement and of the decisive importance of human praxis repeatedly brought this relation into the open.

There surely were grounds for Feuerbach's and Marx's critique. In a more static framework "religion" has been understood and experienced as a special human "faculty", one that enabled man to participate to some extent in the sphere of the supernatural. There have also been tenacious attempts to place it in a dynamic, but polar relation of internal-external, leading to wide-spread use of the word "religiosity" as expression for something increasingly internalized, even anxiously nursed to the degree that the pressure of and impressedness with the "external world" increased; or, conversely, reference to something almost identified with external forms that compensated inner emptiness or uncertainty. All such attempts may well be honest enough, and even undertaken and clung to with intense conviction. We are masters at bending (things) back to ourselves (*"incurvatus in se"*, Luther's telling characterization of our natural effort and life-direction); we are even able to include "religion" – especially religion – in this curvature.

We can try our utmost to correct such notions and to present a more adequate picture. But it seems better, and more necessary today, to drop that overtaxed and soiled word "religion", and to seek a *renewed understanding of powerful biblical words* such as trust, fellowship, expectation, and even "knowledge". This last word taken in so meaningfull a way that it can no longer be opposed to "life" but rather coincides with it, as in: "This is eternal life, that they know Thee...". Words such as these, spoken in utterly concrete and greatly diverse life-situations, such words must once again touch us with all of their meaning and must radiate toward a renewal of our thinking.

2. Relativity of Philosophy

Throughout the book this theme has been in discussion, for the most part in two contexts: a) in connection with presumptuousness concerning the possibilities of philosophy, its self-evident competence to determine or disclose the meaning of human existence both in society and in history (including "nature"), and b) in connection with its dialectic and ambiguous relation to human praxis.

The second problem follows from the first, at least in part. Integration of philosophy within praxis is hampered when that philosophy is already cut loose from the primary relation in which man stands with reality around him – a relation of givenness and acceptance – and instead is constrained, spiderlike, to (re-)construct those relations itself.

This is not to deny that, next to other 19th-century thinkers such as Kierkegaard and Nietzsche, Marx has contributed importantly to a new and sometimes intensive reflection on the relation of philosophy to the whole of (societal) life, its struggles and conflicts, its suffering, its hopes and expectations. Christian thinking cannot afford to leave these realities "in the margin"; it ought to listen, acknowledge their depth, learn from and be moved by them, challenged to appraise its own place and task. Christian thinking can only become humbler that way, but in that humility it can also discern and distinguish more incisively. "More incisively" here also means: with more logical purity, but no longer in the sense of "purely"-logical, nor with a penchant for the artifice "dialectically-logical". The direction in which a christian's life has been set, pregnant with *integration and tension*, is too valuable. He cannot afford to leave his philosophizing out of it in an illusory autonomy, and to let it run stuck in dialectical schematisms.

3. *History*

History can hardly be taken seriously enough. Nowadays this seems a truism. Most philosophical movements and schools show their ever-present awareness of it; some are even obsessed with it. In all kinds of dialogues and discussions there is a strong inclination to relativize standpoints, evaluations, established frameworks and relationships on account of experienced "historicity".

Still, all this is not yet proof that history is really taken seriously. We may become overwhelmed by some reality, and then react in various ways. Man cannot but react. When he lets history wash over him because he has come to experience it as an unaccountable and incomprehensible, but all-embracing Power, he reacts; and this reaction itself contributes to the course of history. Again, it is a reaction when men begin to exploit the discovery of the historical. When, for instance, they seek to encapsulate the most telling traits of relativity, variability, possibility and organization (of things and persons) in a notion of freedom that tips the scales to lust for power and aims at subtle buttressing and escalation of power (a striving that often hides behind talk of "historical laws" and the like). Counterpoint to this reaction is the intentional provocation of anarchy and chaos. But none of these reactions is a sign of what I mean by taking history seriously.

In all this variety of response one basic similarity remains: there is an imposing *datum* to which man reacts, wherewith he must do something; and this, in turn, belongs to the datum itself. This is, I believe, the core of the reality we call history. It is a reality which, from the beginning and without ceasing presents itself to us without our having had a hand in it, but in which we – all of humanity – are embraced and that in this comprehensiveness escapes our conceptualization and definition. Even divine revelation does not stand outside of this history. In the words of a christian thinker:

> This is the amazing character of the sovereign Creator's revelation, *ex origine* transcending man's "conceptual grasp": He brings it to us as *our* history in which we are "interested" – our life depends on it; and yet from out of that history as such it cannot be understood. Neither outside nor through our history can revelation be understood. (J.P.A. Mekkes, *Tijd der Bezinning*; Amsterdam: Buijten en Schipperheijn, 1973, p. 40).

Primary recognition of this history-reality does not mean that the christian is forced to react in one of the ways just sketched. Revelation, as it goes its way through history, teaches the christian two things: a) he learns that nothing is ours to possess. Nothing is the property of any given group or generation. At issue is humanity, "all nations and peoples" who, in history related to one another, are drawn together. And through the ages there is the need for tradition, for handing down and taking along; b) he learns that everything is entrusted to us, i.e., when developed, tested and proven in all its possibilities to be returned to the Giver, so that at last He and we, together with all of it, can enter the Feast.

Indeed, history in this sense pervades everything. Marx, Hegel and others have been aware of this. But all-pervasive is not the same as all-absorbent. Actually, in Marx this is not the case either, witness his need as theoretical thinker to regain and retain a grasp on history; witness also his expectation of and effort towards an historical turning-point, to be achieved through a proletariat "called" to revolution; witness, finally, his fixation on a material "infra-structure" as determining and catalyzing basic factor.

At this point we cannot do without keeping in mind an important distinction. Nothing just *is*, without further ado, at our disposal. Everything calls for disclosure; everything invites or challenges us to investigate, nurture, refine according to the many and varied possibilities. In this process men also "realize" themselves, and thus reveal their variedness. Just now I began with that. But "everything" also means: all sorts of things; numerical structures, for instance, or physical processes, economic and artistic possibilities, jural relationships, etc. In the midst of all these "sorts of things" there is also that which we call "cultural-historical", and which we can briefly point out as being the formable and formative that we meet *in everything* that we touch or do. In everything – that is, this cultural-historical is not something alongside this or that. On the contrary, it is not so that some things or activities could be considered non-historical; and conversely the "cultural-historical" can be understood only in the many-sided and variegated relationships in which it stands to all those structures, processes, relationships etc. mentioned above. Hence there is a "history of . . . " (science, or a specific science, language, politics, art, even furniture, and so on). Now, this "cultural-historical" aspect of things, events, and persons may not be confused or identified with the reality I earlier called "history".

While such confusion or identification is not entirely inexplicable it can really only result from a certain desperation in the face of all-pervasive history, leading either to fatalism or resignation; or else it is inspired by a greed for power that seizes on the cultural-historical in order to have "history" in its grasp. The confusion or identification is indeed understandable since among "all sorts of things" all-pervasive history comes to peculiar expression in the cultural-historical. Here especially the rich possibilities and abundant variety of "all sorts of things" are brought to light. All the same, it is *no more* than expression, and always remains "in the midst of . . . ". That everything (including "nature") is disclosable, in fact is continually being developed via the efforts of men who in this process become increasingly interdependent, but whose praxis is never ended, and that in this way everything moves *towards* something – that is "history" in the universally comprehensive sense.

The christian will guard himself against attempts to encompass or conceptually grasp this history. But he need not collapse under it as under a super force or burden. Everything draws forward. Indeed, nothing less relative or less comprehensive will do. It draws forward, driven by a given primal force that we reverently and without comprehension call "creation". It is a process of unfolding, unfinished, but pregnant with a power that strains towards fulfilment. Viewed in this way, there is no harm in thinking of human experience as a process of learning continued through the generations. Process, however, need not coincide with progress; time and again man has to *un*learn, and that too belongs to the learning-process. Things are not cut and dried; investigation and experiment have a legitimate place. And for the growth of their experience people need each other – that too demands time and effort.

Within the course of history such things do not seem abnormal. But we must notice that especially here evil distortions enter in, and that they are our doing. They take hold especially here, in our having to unlearn so unbelievably much and often, in our not being able to unlearn; in the desperation of "trying", or else, perversely, in our making a cult of it; in misuse of the fact that people and groups of people need others (manipulation via organization). Surely, this is a complicated and bewildering drama.

Similar observations can be made regarding historical "contrasts". These too are not necessarily abnormal. Development often takes place via challenges or under pressures, and these may contain elements of resistance that can be of service to the break-through of new possiblities, new discoveries, and so on. Mutual teaching and nurture and communal organization are never without tensions either. Sometimes a power-struggle is salutary when it takes a great deal of effort, for example, to introduce a new idea. There is such a thing as healthy rivalry.

It is not surprising that philosophers, under the spell of "history", are impressed with these things. Remarkable and significant however is that they industriously and if need be with artifice seek to label these typically historical contrasts as *logical* (or dialectic). This becomes all the more questionable when via this same logic attempts are made to render the scarcely hidden wrongs and corruption attendant upon power-struggles and rivalries more or less "understandable", thereby collaborating in "playing down" evil.

Via the historical we arrive again at history in the comprehensive sense. At that level the christian must indeed recognize a *deepest* contrast. This contrast is an either-or beyond the "logical" or the "historical"; a rivalry Augustine called the battle between the *"civitas terrena"* and the *"civitas Dei"*. Saying this we – carefully! – point to the most incisive and most breath-taking "happening" in heaven and on earth. Let it be done carefully, for whoever says *"civitas Dei"* simultaneously admits that none can *claim* that realm. It is rather God Himself who establishes it – by *giving Himself* and in so doing conferring upon history both focus and goal. By giving Himself: the *"civitas Dei" works* as a *dying* seed! Once christians appropriate this secret, contra revolution *and* conservativism, they will be drawing on and radiating an unprecedented power.

4. *Eschatology and Utopia*

The meaning of history is determined by its goal. That goal has not yet been reached but, as in a journey, conditions every step of the way. Without it history would be overpowering and perplexing in its capriciousness and incomprehensibility; thanks to its goal it reaches ahead, aimed and tensed. This holds for human activity in history also;

amidst all insecurity and uncertainty it moves on, future-directed and by the pull of *expectation*. Cooperative human effort illustrates this more clearly still, since here the factors of insecurity and uncertainty are proportionately greater.

Marx has understood this. Because of this awareness he has held a future-vision of the ultimate destiny of history before the "class" of the proletariat, the legion of revolutionairies and near-communists. Indeed, hope is not an extra addition or pacifier, but rather a fundamental power in our life. It was not just an accident that a twentieth-century neo-Marxist philosopher, Ernst Bloch, wrote his important *Das Prinzip Hoffnung*, nor was it accidental that this publication occasioned the appearance of another important book: *Theologie der Hoffnung* (J. Moltmann). Christians and Marxists have something in common here.

Nevertheless, on just this point there is an unmistakable difference too. It is not to be clarified in a few words. Actually, the real difference is not so much a matter for clarification; much rather it is a matter of existentially experiencing and doing. It may well be that one of the most significant challenges confronting contemporary christians is to demonstrate bodily what *living* in and out of hope can be and mean; "to be saved in it"; "to be reborn to a living hope" (Rom. 8 : 24; 1 Peter 1 : 3).

But this is a book, and so, because of the relevance and importance of the matter at hand, a brief attempt at formulation must be made. Without using very strict, theoretical terms just yet, we may note two things:

1) Marx and his followers have always managed to combine a marked orientation to the future with an equally unwavering agitation and defense of violence. On account of their hope christians have rejected violence. I am not thinking of those "christians" who thought their best interest served if the existing situation were maintained, not to mention those who collaborated in repression; nor am I thinking of those who passively acquiesced to a "fate". I think of those who learned the *power of suffering*, and made it their eloquent witness.

2) If one reads Marx attentively, one can hear an undertone of desperation. To be sure, the voice of robust militancy and indignation dominates. But there is detectable also something of the flailing movements of one about to drown, one who has lost contact with a hitherto well-known bottom and who now gropes about seeking a new foothold. In some respects Marx is not unlike prophets of doom such as Kierkegaard, Burckhardt and Nietzsche. Among some neo-Marxists today – and these not the lesser figures among them (Horkheimer, Adorno) – despair has become more than just an undertone. Christians should not be deaf to this. The brute massivity of most revolutionary violence

to which I pointed earlier has a hollowness and weakness to it. The christian hope for the future also means that desperation is overcome, no matter how many riddles remain. The christian hope gives birth to an experience of deliverance. This is no mere contentment; even less is it smugness, but rather a tensed and taut look-out for Someone to come. Someone busy drawing everyone to Himself. Indeed, in hope our life gets its true tension and resilience. At the same time it is here, just here, that the real, often wordless testing of convictions takes place.

Speaking more theoretically we can make use of the terms Eschatology and Utopia. In our time utopian thinking has witnessed a revival. In Marx it is present as well, be it in rudimentary form. The revival in utopian thinking witnesses to the elasticity and resilience of the human selfhood, reaching towards a destiny not yet achieved but constituting a determinant in the present. Especially at the beginning of the modern period and at its end (the current period) markedly utopian tendencies come to light. During the first phase utopia is largely the product of a strong and sometimes almost unlimited optimism; it is a utopia that makes manifest the break-through of existing boundaries, the yearning for the in-finite. Today utopian thinking is no less authentic but reminds us more of the outstretched arms of one drowning. In neither attitude there is any notion of letting oneself be pulled up and led along by another arm, by a proferred hand that is to be grasped and held on to for dear life.

Here lies the decisive difference with what we conceptually call "eschatology". It is not a matter of quietistic rest instead of dynamic movement or of acceptance over against unceasing effort. The hand that is grasped and held is covered with scars and precisely because of that one has learned to recognize and trust it. No-one, not the christian either, gets the chance to settle; there is no chance even to climb a raft to gain a bearing on the torrents and rapids ahead. But there is a real magnetic pull; the pull of a Hand that draws us, not out of but through history's currents. That to which our weak word "eschatology" would point has been incomparably formulated by the apostle Paul when he spoke of the entire universe groaning as if in the pangs of childbirth (Romans 8). Utopias pale in comparison with strains and shocks so necessary, so profound, so true to life, and so universal.

Living eschatologically is the strength and endurance to see scars turn into signs of things to come. It is no more. The christian owns no divining rod or crystal ball. The planning and carrying out of violent revolutions is often the practical side of the theoretically designed utopian coin, or else an angry, desperate reaction to it. (In *Utopia and Violence*, and *The Open Society and Its Enemies* Karl Popper has made some pointed remarks in this connection, even though they are not always equally profound). Both sides of the coin have this in common: people trying to (face-)lift the future and so overreaching themselves. The resultant tension is a wildly swinging pendulum between present and future. But to participate in a "pregnant present" – in the sense of Paul's words – in which the future is irresistibly making its way, to undergo and consciously experience the convulsions, the shocks and pains of it – that is something else altogether.

One last question. Can a man endure this lack of insight and over-view? Is it not true that the recognition of this "lack" limits his possibilities? That depends. There are contemporary philosophical schools in which the "hiddenness" of history has become a central theme. Oddly enough, this too is meant as a reaction to christendom which, such thinkers hold, would (claim to) know too much. I trust that it is sufficiently clear that I do not feel at home in that kind of christendom. In history hiddenness is indeed far more than an added feature. It is no mere hampering epi-phenomenon that can be gotten rid of by violent revolutionary or utopian or dialectic means. On the other hand, it is no phenomenon before which one's "historical reason" or practical "resignation" must bow. A christian view of history must reckon seriously with things hidden, but this because they are announced by Him who leads history and who has bound himself historically to mankind, via this announcement, for instance. Such communication is meant to increase the respect for Him who leads, to be sure, but even more to intensify our concentration upon that which has already been revealed ("to do this" – today), and to heighten the tensed expectation of marvels that this Ally still has in store for us.

Again: exposition must necessarily fall short; more and more it will be the crucible of living it that counts.

5. *"Nature"*

We know that the demythologizing and desacralizing of the "concept" of nature is in part a Jewish and christian heritage. In this way room was created for man's far-reaching exploration of and control over natural processes. But time and time again man, existing bodily even in his boldest thoughts and proudest designs, has had to recognize that he is in every part but molded of earthly clay. Tensions were inevitable. The great Immanuel Kant once summarized the cardinal issue of his thinking as the problem-complex of "nature and freedom". Threatening depletion of our natural resources and multiple environmental pollu-tion have nowadays caused many to be genuinely alarmed. There is an evident tendency – born of reaction – to call "technology" the responsible monster, and to crown "nature" with a romantic halo.

Attempts are even made to become "one with nature" again, to loose one-self in it. Marx did not join this quest. He was satisfied with a "metabolism" between man and nature. In his double idea of the "naturalization of man" and the "humanization of nature" the central idea of the self-productivity of the human species actually remained untouched; in this process nature plays an important, but "mediating" role.

It seems to me high time for christians to reconsider their understanding of their bond to nature. All too easily they often assimilated technical acquisitions, believing themselves justified by the demythology and desacralization mentioned above. Well, that heritage is ours and cannot be denied. There is no need of neo-paganism, nor of a new romanticism of nature. Expressions such as "the green hell", "the scorching sun", etc., do originate in basic experiences. And to the extent that man, only man, can reduce the sting of such experiences he is called to do so. It is indeed true that nature, which permeates man from head to toe, is also *entrusted* to him, to *work with*. What possibilities, and what a risk! In order to really come to a working with nature, rather than exploiting or idolizing it, the primary and recurrent act demanded of us is this: to let the mysteriousness of this basic datum come to our full awareness. This is no nature-mysticism. What I mean is that "nature" contains abundance, endless variation, at the same time a wordless rythm and regularity that renders us speechless and so atunes us and all our instrumentation to a finer and more receptive hearing of the creative, meaninggiving *Word*, the Word that calls man to responsible stewardship.

In "nature" creation reveals itself as *given*ness, overpowering without being obtrusive. We ourselves are fitted into it, as we most impressively feel in our emotions, our impulsiveness, moods and habits, including every subtle nuance and all unreflected, wordless accuracy that accompany these – the miracle of our "psychical" life.

Nature and freedom – let us go back a moment to this classical formulation. In spite of all the unanswered questions the christian can see no sense in playing the one off against the other, or in assigning a limited realm to each. Undoubtedly, there is much in nature that is a means for our responsible action. But the natural is not just "means", it surrounds us, carries and regulates us in our every activity, it enchants and bewilders us. It is, not least in its tiniest micro-structures, too great and too awesome to be mere "means". Conversely, it will not lend itself – certainly not in the long run – to pathetic worship (intoxication) or to fatalistic acceptance (blind, capricious, but inexorable "contingency"). For that too, nature is too awe-inspiring, but even more: too penetrating, too constant, too speechless. Nature gives no answer – we do that. Nature demands it and insists on it.

Perhaps we can formulate as follows: in its unity of stability-and-abundance nature is the pre-condition for meaningul freedom. As *pre*-condition it is ever present and around human life – powerful, but also inviting (often challenging) to more, to action. As pre-*condition* it constitutes the continuous reminder of intrinsic dependence and given-ness. At the same time this is a healthy obstacle to our propensity to unhitch our conditions and values from nature by letting them arise out of our "creativity". The natural power operative in our psychical life ("force", "reinforcement") is real. It is something that plays its part in our acceptance of norms, in our being motivated by them; it is a power than can perhaps be characterized as a *transition* to the "normative". The value of this power is that it cooperates in the concrete stabilization of my responsible action, and ensures that this action – as such more than psychical – remains concretely related to every variation and nuance around me to which I can be sensitive.

6. *Labor*

In conclusion just a few remarks on "labor". No more than that, for this topic touches on a great many extremely complicated social issues.

Labor is not that which makes a man human, that by which he is enabled to produce himself according to his worth, and "division" of which would necessarily detract from that authenticity and worth. Nor is labor a mere instrument, an unavoidable means (or "evil") in service of "survival". Labor is necessary, to be sure, but it is also a magnificent mission. Labor is a mission that fits us so well that we ought to be able to disclose and unfold our humanity in it. There is a great deal wrong with the opportunities to fulfil our calling so understood, especially in the existing organization of labor and in factual cooperation. There is even much that runs counter to such possibilities. But a correction of that situation will have to derive its motivation from the thesis above, and not from one of the rejected views.

In practice these views have not stood the test. Neither the elevation of the laborer to the status of ideal man, nor his degradation to a cog in the technico-economical wheels is seriously adhered to any longer, and is nowhere defended. Since Marx and partly because of him improvements have come, not without struggle. But one may fear that much real correction does not materialize because the relationship between "employers" and "employees" has more or less taken on the character of a political power-struggle. It is to be feared that responses to this will continue to be reactionary, and therefore unable to effectuate a real break-through. What are we to say, for instance, when some neo-Marxists plead for a truly human – political – "interaction", contrasted with and surpassing "labor", technologically conceived? The intentions are understandable and to some degree to be applauded. But on the one hand adherence to a technicistic concept of labor leaves too much unscathed, and on the other hand the plea for a politicizing of our humanity is, at best, a crippled and naive testimony to a longing for true human communication (dialogue). This is not to say that I think political consciousness unimportant. I consider it sufficiently important to regard the word "citizen" as a title of honor, and to have difficulties with the word "extra-parlementary action", whether it be used by adherent or dissident. However: a) active participation in society on the part of the greatest possible number of people does not coincide with the political power-struggle, and b) active participation in society is more embracing than participation in things political; and this is a good thing, good also for the political.

One more reactionary attitude merits mention. This is a reaction against misunderstood or factually devaluated labor and against the turn to politics both. I mean the praise of play. Work and play is a current, though hardly novel theme. It is a many-faceted theme that obviously cannot be "dealt with" here. But with an eye to its timeliness, and in view of the element of reaction in it I add a brief note.

Much good can be said about play. It is decidedly not just something incidental in human existence, but rather it is deeply rooted in it; at bottom a reference to the play-fulness of Wisdom itself, prior to and during the divine work (Proverbs 8). Playfulness is universal. All sorts of human activities can, and even should, witness to the playful element. Does this allow us to play playfulness off against labor, or to let it take precedence? I think not. The circumstance that all sorts of human activities may display this element does not imply that everything become or need become "play". It is only in concrete games that this element *dominates*. And concrete games (in great variety) certainly have a positive function of their own; namely, the testing and enjoyable shaping of human capabilities; we can even train ourselves in them. But games for which we train, relaxing as they are meant to be, demand effort – and in labor it is effort that dominates. We can speak of a rythm of work and play. At least, that's the way it should be.

There is, then, no reason to oppose the one to the other. But again, the reaction in which this is done is understandable. In many activities and relationships we have lost a healthy "being at ease". Salutary boundaries have become stifling bonds. Labor costs sweat and yields disillusion. But whoever thinks that "play" is able to overcome this brokenness and tension is only fooling himself. For a while it may bring solace, but it too is hardly resistent to similar disturbances; only too soon it degenerates into illusion or obsession! Our play too needs deliverance.